STEP-BY-STEP

COMPLETE
Chinese
COOKING

STEP-BY-STEP

COMPLETE

Chinese

COOKING

DEH-TA HSIUNG

WENDY LEE

First published in Great Britain in 1995 by
Parragon
Unit 13–17
Avonbridge Trading Estate
Atlantic Road
Avonmouth
Bristol BS11 9QD

Copyright © Parragon 1995

Reprinted in 1997

ISBN 0-7525-0131-3

Printed in Italy

Acknowledgements:
Art Direction: Ron Samuels
Editors: Beverly LeBlanc, Diana Vowles
Design: Somewhere Creative
Photography: Amanda Heywood, Joff Lee
Home Economists: Deh-Ta Hsiung, Wendy Lee
Styling: John Lee Studios, Marian Price

Photographs on pages 12, 24, 32, 62 and 72 reproduced by permission of Tony Stone Images; on pages 84, 96, 108, 124, 140, 156, 168, 178, 190 and 208 reproduced by permission of ZEFA Picture Library (UK) Ltd.

Material contained in this book has previously appeared in *Chinese Cantonese Cooking, Vegetarian Chinese Cooking* and *Chinese Szechuan Cooking.*

Note:
Cup measurements in this book are for American cups. Tablespoons are assumed to be 15ml. Unless otherwise stated, milk is assumed to be full-fat, eggs are standard size 2 and pepper is freshly ground black pepper.

Contents

COMPLETE
Chinese
COOKING

The cuisine of China is varied and diverse.
Each region has different specialities, such as
the hot, spicy dishes of the Szechuan region,
and the aromatic crispy duck from Beijing. In
Chinese cuisine, the emphasis is on a balance
of flavours, aromas, textures and colours in
each meal. Many dishes are simple to
prepare, and all are delicious.

This colourful and comprehensive selection
of recipes from the different regions of China
provides a glorious range of exotic dishes,
with step-by-step instructions showing how
to prepare each one. Over the following
pages, discover how to create these elegant
and delicious dishes in your own kitchen to
serve as exciting everyday meals or as
special-occasion dinners to delight your
guests.

1

CANTONESE COOKING

CHAPTER ONE

Appetizers

A number of dishes in Cantonese cooking are served as an appetizer – just like hors d'oeuvres in the West. One of the advantages of these dishes is that they are generally prepared and cooked well in advance – hours or even days before serving. Also, almost all the dishes selected here are ideal for a buffet-style meal or as party food.

Instead of serving different appetizers individually, try serving a small portion of each together as an assorted hors d'oeuvres. Select a minimum of three or four different items: Crispy Spring (Egg) Rolls, Butterfly Prawns (Shrimps), Barbecue Spare Ribs, Barbecue Pork (Char Siu), and so on.

Other dishes from the Main Course section that can be served as a part of the appetizer are Sweet and Sour Prawns (Shrimps), Lemon Chicken, and Baked Crab with Ginger and Spring Onions (Scallions). Remember not to have more than one of the same type of food – the ingredients should be chosen for their harmony and balance in colour, aroma, flavour and texture.

Opposite: A Chinese cook at an open-air stall in Xinjiang province. Wayside stalls selling takeaway food are a common sight all over China, offering wontons, spare ribs, prawns (shrimp), spring (egg) rolls and other tasty snacks for hungry workers.

STEP 3

STEP 4

STEP 5

STEP 6

CRISPY VEGETARIAN SPRING (EGG) ROLLS

For a non-vegetarian version, just replace mushrooms with chicken or pork, and the carrots with prawns (shrimps).

MAKES 12 ROLLS

125 g/4 oz/2 cups fresh bean-sprouts,
  washed and drained
60 g/2 oz spring onions (scallions)
60 g/2 oz carrots
60 g/2 oz canned sliced bamboo shoots,
  rinsed and drained
60 g/2 oz mushrooms
2–3 tbsp vegetable oil, plus oil for deep-frying
$^{1}/_{2}$ tsp salt
$^{1}/_{2}$ tsp sugar
1 tbsp light soy sauce
1 tsp Chinese rice wine or dry sherry
12 spring (egg) roll skins, defrosted if frozen
1 tbsp cornflour (cornstarch) paste (see page
  231)
flour for dusting
vegetable oil for deep-frying

1 Cut all the vegetables into thin shreds roughly the same size and shape as the bean-sprouts.

2 Heat the oil in a preheated wok and stir-fry the vegetables for about 1 minute. Add the salt, sugar, soy sauce and wine and continue stirring for 1½–2 minutes. Remove the vegetables from the wok with a slotted spoon and place in a bowl. Drain off the excess liquid then leave to cool.

3 To make the spring (egg) rolls, place about 2 tablespoons of the vegetables one-third of the way down on a spring (egg) roll skin, with the triangle pointing away from you.

4 Lift the lower flap over the filling and fold in one end.

5 Roll once and fold in the other end to completely enclose the filling.

6 Roll once more, brush the upper edge with a little cornflour (cornstarch) paste, and roll into a neat package. Lightly dust a tray with flour and place the spring (egg) roll with the flap-side down. Make the remaining spring (egg) rolls the same .

7 Heat the oil in a preheated wok or deep-fryer until smoking, then reduce the heat to low and deep-fry the spring (egg) rolls in batches for 2–3 minutes or until golden and crispy. Remove with a slotted spoon and drain on paper towels. Serve hot with a dipping sauce, such as soy sauce, sweet and sour sauce or chilli sauce, which you can buy at the supermarket.

BUTTERFLY PRAWNS (SHRIMP)

Use unpeeled, raw king or tiger prawns (or jumbo shrimp) which are about 7–10 cm/3–4 inches long.

STEP 1

SERVES 4

12 raw tiger prawns (or jumbo shrimp) in
  their shells
2 tbsp light soy sauce
1 tbsp Chinese rice wine or dry sherry
1 tbsp cornflour (cornstarch)
2 eggs, lightly beaten
8–10 tbsp breadcrumbs
vegetable oil for deep-frying
salt and pepper
shredded lettuce leaves, to serve
chopped spring onions (scallions), to garnish

1 Peel and devein the prawns
(shrimp) but leave the tails on. Split
them in half from the underbelly about
halfway along, leaving the tails still
firmly attached.

2 Mix together the salt, pepper, soy
sauce, wine and cornflour
(cornstarch) in a bowl, add the prawns
(shrimp) and turn to coat. Leave to
marinate for 10–15 minutes.

3 Heat the oil in a preheated wok.
Pick up each prawn (shrimp) by
the tail, dip it in the beaten egg then roll
it in the breadcrumbs to coat well.

4 Deep-fry the prawns (shrimp) in
batches until golden brown.
Remove them with a slotted spoon and
drain on paper towels.

5 To serve, arrange the prawns
(shrimp) neatly on a bed of lettuce
leaves and garnish with spring onions
(scallions), either raw or soaked for about
30 seconds in hot oil.

VARIATIONS

Butterfly prawns (shrimp) may also be
served on a bed of crispy seaweed (see
page 88). This classic Chinese accompaniment provides the perfect foil for the
luscious prawns (shrimp). Dried seaweed
can be bought in packets from Oriental
food stores and supermarkets. Follow the
instructions on the packet to prepare it.

TO DEVEIN LARGE PRAWNS (SHRIMP)

First remove the shell. Make a shallow cut
about three-quarters of the way along the
back of each prawn (shrimp), then pull out
and discard the black intestinal vein.

STEP 1

STEP 3

STEP 3

STEP 1

STEP 2

STEP 3

STEP 4

LETTUCE-WRAPPED MINCED (GROUND) MEAT

*The original version of this recipe uses quail or pigeon meat.
Serve the minced (ground) meat and lettuce leaves on separate dishes;
each guest then wraps his or her own parcel.*

SERVES 4

*250 g/8 oz minced (ground) pork or chicken
1 tbsp finely chopped Chinese mushrooms
1 tbsp finely chopped water chestnuts
salt and pepper
pinch sugar
1 tsp light soy sauce
1 tsp Chinese rice wine or dry sherry
1 tsp cornflour (cornstarch)
2–3 tbsp vegetable oil
1/2 tsp finely chopped ginger root
1 tsp finely chopped spring onions
    (scallions)
1 tbsp finely chopped Szechuan preserved
    vegetables (optional)
1 tbsp oyster sauce
a few drops sesame oil
8 crisp lettuce leaves, to serve*

1 Mix the minced (ground) meat with the mushrooms, water chestnuts, salt, pepper, sugar, soy sauce, wine and cornflour (cornstarch).

2 Heat the oil in a preheated wok or frying pan (skillet). Add the ginger and spring onions (scallions) followed by the meat. Stir-fry for 1 minute.

3 Add the Szechuan preserved vegetables and continue stirring for 1 more minute. Add the oyster sauce and sesame oil, blend well and cook for 1 more minute. Remove to a warmed serving dish.

4 To serve: place 2–3 tablespoons of the mixture on a lettuce leaf and roll it up tightly to form a small parcel. Eat with your fingers.

SZECHUAN PRESERVED VEGETABLES

These pickled mustard roots are hot and salty, with a peppery flavour, and are often used to intensify the spiciness of a dish. Once opened, store in the refrigerator in a tightly sealed jar.

STEP 1

STEP 2

STEP 3

STEP 4

BARBECUE SPARE RIBS

This is a simplified version of the half saddle of pork ribs seen hanging in the windows of Cantonese restaurants. Use the specially small, thin ribs known as finger ribs.

SERVES 4
OVEN: 230°C/450°F/GAS MARK 8;
THEN 200°C/400°F/GAS MARK 6

500 g/1 lb pork finger spare ribs
1 tbsp sugar
1 tbsp light soy sauce
1 tbsp dark soy sauce
3 tbsp hoi-sin sauce
1 tbsp rice wine or dry sherry
4–5 tbsp water or Chinese Stock (see page 230)
mild chilli sauce, to dip
coriander (cilantro) leaves, to garnish

1 Trim off any excess fat from the ribs and cut into pieces. Mix the ribs with the sugar, light and dark soy sauces, hoi-sin sauce and wine in a baking dish, and marinate for 2–3 hours.

2 Add the water or stock to the ribs and spread them out in the dish. Roast in a preheated hot oven for 15 minutes.

3 Turn the ribs over, lower the heat and continue roasting for 30–35 minutes longer.

4 To serve, chop each rib into 3–4 small, bite-sized pieces with a large knife or Chinese cleaver and arrange on a serving dish. Pour the sauce from the baking dish over them, garnish with coriander (cilantro) leaves, and serve with chilli sauce as a dip.

HOI-SIN SAUCE

This sweet, thick sauce is made from soybean flour, soy beans, vinegar, sesame seed oil, chilli, sugar, salt, garlic and spices. It is sold in cans and jars; if you buy it in a can, store it in a glass bottle in the refrigerator once opened, where it will keep for several months. It is ideal for use in marinades and as a dip or condiment for many Chinese dishes.

SPARE RIBS

Ask your local butcher to cut some if you can't find the right size of ribs in the supermarket. Don't throw away any trimmings from the ribs – they can be used for soup or stock.

STEP 1

STEP 2

STEP 4

STEP 5

BARBECUE PORK (CHAR SIU)

Also called honey-roasted pork, these are the strips of reddish meat sometimes seen hanging in the windows of Cantonese restaurants.

SERVES 4
OVEN: 220°C/425°F/GAS MARK 7;
THEN 180°C/350°F/GAS MARK 4

500 g/1 lb pork fillet (tenderloin)
150 ml/¹/₄ pint/²/₃ cup boiling water
1 tbsp honey, dissolved with a little hot
*   water*
shredded lettuce, to serve

MARINADE:
1 tbsp sugar
1 tbsp crushed yellow bean sauce
1 tbsp light soy sauce
1 tbsp hoi-sin sauce
1 tbsp oyster sauce
¹/₂ tsp chilli sauce
1 tbsp brandy or rum
1 tsp sesame oil

1 Cut the pork into strips about 2.5 cm/1 inch thick and 18–20 cm/7–8 inch long and place in a large shallow dish. Add the marinade ingredients and turn the pork until well coated. Cover and leave to marinate for at least 3–4 hours, turning occasionally.

2 Remove the pork strips from the dish with a slotted spoon, reserving the marinade. Arrange the pork strips on a rack over a baking tin (pan). Place the tin (pan) in the preheated oven and pour in the boiling water. Roast for about 10–15 minutes.

3 Lower the oven temperature. Baste the pork strips with the reserved marinade and turn. Roast for a further 10 minutes.

4 Remove the pork from the oven, brush with the honey syrup, and lightly brown under a medium-hot grill (broiler) for 3–4 minutes, turning them over once or twice.

5 To serve, allow the pork to cool slightly before cutting it. Cut across the grain into thin slices and arrange on a bed of shredded lettuce. Make a sauce by boiling the marinade and the drippings in the baking tin (pan) for a few minutes, strain and pour over the pork.

CHAPTER TWO

Soups

Soup is not normally served as a separate course in China, except at formal occasions and banquets – and then it usually appears towards the end of the meal.

At an everyday meal in Chinese homes, a simply made soup, almost always a clear broth in which a small amount of thinly sliced or shredded vegetables and/or meat have been poached quickly, is served with the other dishes in the meal.

If a good stock is not available, as is often the case in Chinese homes, a Chinese housewife would just stir-fry the ingredients first in a little oil, then add water and seasonings (salt, soy sauce or monosodium glutamate) to make an instant soup fit for the gods!

If you use a chicken stock cube, remember to reduce the amount of seasonings in the recipes, since most commercially-made stock cubes are fairly salty and spicy. It is always worth making your own Chinese Stock (see page 230) if you have the time.

Opposite: *Father and son enjoy a bowl of soup with wontons in a Shanghai restaurant. In China soup is usually served with other dishes as part of a meal, not a separate course as in the West.*

SWEETCORN (CORN) & CRAB MEAT SOUP

You must use American-style creamed sweetcorn (corn) for this soup since it originated in the USA! Chicken can be used instead of the crab meat, if preferred.

STEP 1

STEP 2

STEP 3

STEP 4

SERVES 4

125 g/4 oz crab meat
¼ tsp finely chopped ginger root
2 egg whites
2 tbsp milk
1 tbsp cornflour (cornstarch) paste (see page 231)
600 ml/1 pint/2 ½ cups Chinese Stock (see page 230)
250 g/8 oz can American-style creamed sweetcorn (corn)
salt and pepper
finely chopped spring onions (scallions), to garnish

1 Flake the crab meat (or coarsely chop the chicken breast) and mix with the ginger.

2 Beat the egg whites until frothy, add the milk and cornflour (cornstarch) paste and beat again until smooth. Blend in the crab or chicken.

3 In a wok or large frying pan (skillet), bring the stock to the boil, add the creamed sweetcorn (corn) and bring back to the boil.

4 Stir in the crab meat or chicken pieces and egg-white mixture, adjust the seasoning and stir gently until the mixture is well blended. Serve hot, garnished with chopped spring onions (scallions).

CHOOSING CRAB

Always buy the freshest possible crab; fresh is best, though frozen or canned will work for this recipe. The delicate, sweet flavour of crab diminishes quickly: this is why many Chinese cooks make a point of buying live crabs.

CREAMED SWEETCORN

Although sweetcorn (corn) is not unknown in Asia today, it really is a Western food by tradition. Be sure to use proper creamed sweetcorn (corn) for this soup, as it has quite a different texture from the more usual sweetcorn (corn) kernels. Creamed sweetcorn (corn) has a thick, slightly mushy consistency, making a thick, creamy soup.

STEP 1

STEP 2

STEP 3

STEP 5

SEAFOOD & TOFU (BEAN CURD) SOUP

Use prawn (shrimp), squid or scallops, or a combination of all three.

SERVES 4

250 g/8 oz seafood, such as peeled prawns (shrimp), squid or scallops, defrosted if frozen
½ egg white, lightly beaten
1 tbsp cornflour (cornstarch) paste (see page 231)
1 cake tofu (bean curd)
750 ml/1¼ pints/3 cups Chinese Stock (see page 230)
1 tbsp light soy sauce
salt and pepper
fresh coriander (cilantro) leaves, to garnish

1 Small prawns (shrimp) can be left whole; larger ones should be cut into smaller pieces; cut the squid and scallops into small pieces.

2 If raw, mix the prawns (shrimp) and scallops with the egg white and cornflour (cornstarch) paste to prevent them from becoming tough

3 Cut the cake of tofu (bean curd) into about 24 small cubes.

4 Bring the stock to a rolling boil. Add the tofu (bean curd) and soy sauce, bring back to the boil and simmer for 1 minute.

5 Stir in the seafood, raw pieces first, pre-cooked ones last. Bring back to the boil and simmer for just 1 minute. Adjust the seasoning and serve garnished with fresh coriander (cilantro) leaves, if liked.

FRESH CORIANDER (CILANTRO)

The musky, sharp scent and flavour of fresh coriander (cilantro) is truly distinctive. When buying it fresh, look for bright green, unwilted leaves. To store it, wash and dry the leaves and leave them on the stem. Wrap the leaves in damp paper towels and keep them in a plastic bag in the refrigerator.

TOFU

Tofu, also known as bean curd, is an almost tasteless substance made from puréed yellow soya beans which are very high in protein. It is widely available in supermarkets, and Oriental and health-food stores. It is sold in cakes about 7.5 cm / 3 inches square.

STEP 1

STEP 2

STEP 3

STEP 4

MIXED VEGETABLE SOUP

*Select three or four of the suggested vegetables for this soup: the
Chinese like to blend different colours, flavours and textures in order to
create harmony as well as contrast.*

SERVES 4

*about 30–60 g / 1–2 oz each of mushrooms,
carrots, asparagus, mangetout (snow
peas), bamboo shoots, baby corns,
cucumber, tomatoes, spinach, lettuce,
Chinese leaves, tofu (bean curd), etc.*
*600 ml / 1 pint / 2 ½ cups Chinese Stock (see
page 230)*
1 tbsp light soy sauce
a few drops sesame oil (optional)
salt and pepper
*finely chopped spring onions (scallions), to
garnish*

1 Cut your selection of vegetables
into roughly uniform shapes
(slices, shreds or cubes) and sizes.

2 Bring the stock to a rolling boil in a
wok and add the vegetables,
bearing in mind that some require a
longer cooking time than others: add
carrots and baby corns first, cook for 2
minutes, then add asparagus,
mushrooms, Chinese leaves, tofu (bean
curd), and cook for another minute.

3 Spinach, lettuce, watercress,
cucumber and tomato are added
last. Stir and bring the soup back to
the boil.

4 Add soy sauce and the sesame oil,
and adjust the seasoning. Serve
hot, garnished with spring onions
(scallions).

SESAME OIL

Sesame oil is a low-saturate oil widely
used for its nutty, aromatic flavour. This
rich-flavoured oil is made from toasted
sesame seeds and used as a seasoning,
not as a cooking oil. Thick and dark, it
burns easily, so it should be added at the
last moment, just before serving. It makes
a wonderful dressing for salads when
diluted with other vegetable oils. A few
drops are often added to soups and other
dishes just before serving – it can often be
seen floating on the surface, as in the
photograph opposite.

CHAPTER THREE

Main Course Dishes

The main course dishes in a conventional Chinese meal are usually stir-fried or braised. Certain dishes may require a longer cooking time and, strictly speaking, belong to a separate course – known as the principal dish – and should be served independently.

Stir-frying meat and fish dishes have become very popular in Western kitchens in recent years. This is because these dishes are comparatively simple and easy to prepare and cook, as well as being economical, delicious and healthy. Basically, the ingredients are cut into small, thin slices or shreds, then tossed and stirred in hot oil over high heat for a very short time. Thus the natural flavours, as well as the subtle textures, of the ingredients are preserved. When correctly done, the meats (which include fish and poultry) should be tender and juicy, and the vegetables crisp and bright – overcooking will render the food into a tasteless soggy mess.

Opposite: Work is finished for the day, and a cook in XinJiang sells noodles for the evening meal. It takes years to learn the art of making noodles and the products of specialist noodle-makers are greatly sought after.

STEP 1

STEP 2

STEP 3

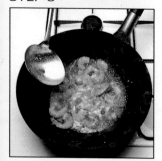

STEP 4

SWEET & SOUR PRAWNS (SHRIMP)

Use raw prawns (shrimp) if possible; ready-cooked ones can be added to the sauce without the initial deep-frying (step 2).

SERVES 4

*300–350 g/10–12 oz raw king or tiger
   prawns (or jumbo shrimp) in their shells
vegetable oil for deep-frying
fresh coriander (cilantro) leaves, to garnish*

*SAUCE:
1 tbsp vegetable oil
2 tsp finely chopped spring onions
   (scallions)
1 tsp finely chopped ginger root
1 tbsp light soy sauce
2 tbsp sugar
3 tbsp rice vinegar
1 tsp Chinese rice wine or dry sherry
125 ml/4 fl oz/1/2 cup Chinese Stock (see
   page 230) or water
1 tbsp cornflour (cornstarch) paste (see
   page 231)
a few drops sesame oil
coriander (cilantro) leaves, to garnish*

1 Remove the legs from the prawns (shrimp) but leave the body shells.

2 Heat the oil in a preheated wok. Deep-fry the prawns (shrimp) in the hot oil for about 45–50 seconds, or until they become bright orange. Remove with a slotted spoon and drain well on paper towels.

3 To make the sauce, heat the oil in a preheated wok and add the spring onions (scallions) and ginger, followed by the seasonings, sugar and stock or water. Bring to the boil.

4 Add the prawns (shrimp) to the sauce, blend well, then thicken the sauce with the cornflour (cornstarch) paste. Stir until smooth and add the sesame oil.

5 Serve hot, garnished with fresh coriander (cilantro) leaves.

SWEET & SOUR SAUCE

It is now possible to buy sweet and sour sauce in bottles. They are really handy if you are short of time, but they are no match for the homemade version, which has a much subtler flavour.

STEP 2

STEP 3

STEP 4

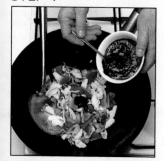

STEP 5

FRIED SQUID FLOWERS

The addition of green (bell) pepper and black bean sauce to the squid makes a colourful and delicious dish from the Cantonese school.

SERVES 4

350–400 g/12–14 oz prepared and cleaned
    squid (see below right)
1 medium green (bell) pepper, cored and
    deseeded
3–4 tbsp vegetable oil
1 garlic clove, finely chopped
¼ tsp finely chopped ginger root
2 tsp finely chopped spring onions
    (scallions)
½ tsp salt
2 tbsp crushed black bean sauce
1 tsp Chinese rice wine or dry sherry
a few drops sesame oil

1 If ready-prepared squid is not available, prepare as instructed in the box, below right.

2 Open up the squid and score the inside of the flesh in a criss-cross pattern with a cleaver or kitchen knife.

3 Cut the squid into pieces about the size of an oblong postage stamp. Blanch in a bowl of boiling water for a few seconds. Remove and drain; dry well on paper towels.

4 Cut the (bell) pepper into small triangular pieces. Heat the oil in a preheated wok. Stir-fry the (bell) pepper for about 1 minute. Add the garlic, ginger, spring onion (scallion), salt and squid. Continue stir-frying for another minute.

5 Finally add the black bean sauce and wine, and blend well. Serve hot, sprinkled with sesame oil.

TO CLEAN THE SQUID

Clean the squid by first cutting off the head. Cut off the tentacles and reserve. Remove the small soft bone at the base of the tentacles and the transparent backbone, as well as the ink bag. Peel off the thin skin, then wash and dry well.

CANTONESE STIR-FRIED PRAWNS (SHRIMP)

This colourful and delicious dish is cooked with vegetables: vary them according to seasonal availability.

STEP 1

SERVES 4

60 g/2 oz mangetout (snow peas)
½ small carrot, thinly sliced
60 g/2 oz baby corns
60 g/2 oz straw mushrooms
175–250 g/6–8 oz raw tiger prawns (or jumbo shrimp), peeled
1 tsp salt
½ egg white, lightly beaten
1 tsp cornflour (cornstarch) paste (see page 231)
about 300ml/½ pint/1¼ cups vegetable oil
1 spring onion (scallion), cut into short sections
4 slices ginger root, peeled and finely chopped
½ tsp sugar
1 tbsp light soy sauce
1 tsp Chinese rice wine or dry sherry
a few drops sesame oil

1 Top and tail the mangetout (snow peas); cut the carrot into the same size as the mangetout (snow peas); halve the baby sweetcorn and straw mushrooms.

2 Mix the prawns (shrimp) with a pinch of the salt, the egg white and cornflour (cornstarch) paste.

3 Heat a wok over high heat for 2–3 minutes, then add the oil and heat to medium-hot before adding the prawns (shrimp); stir to separate them. Remove with a slotted spoon as soon as the colour changes.

4 Pour off the oil, leaving about 1 tablespoon in the wok. Add all the vegetables and stir-fry for about 1 minute. Add the prawns (shrimp) and the seasonings. Blend well. Sprinkle with the sesame oil and serve hot.

STEP 2

STEP 3

VEGETABLE SELECTION

When choosing alternative vegetables, remember to select contrasting colours and textures, as shown here – one green, one orange, one yellow, etc.

STEP 4

STEP 1

STEP 2

STEP 3

STEP 4

BAKED CRAB WITH GINGER

The crab is interchangeable with lobster. In Chinese restaurants, only live crabs and lobsters are used, but ready-cooked ones can be used at home quite successfully.

SERVES 4

1 large or 2 medium crabs, weighing about
    750 g/ 1¹/₂ lb in total
2 tbsp Chinese rice wine or dry sherry
1 egg, lightly beaten
1 tbsp cornflour (cornstarch)
3–4 tbsp vegetable oil
1 tbsp finely chopped ginger root
3-4 spring onions (scallions), cut into sections
2 tbsp light soy sauce
1 tsp sugar
about 75 ml/ 5 tbsp/¹/₃ cup Chinese Stock (see
    page 230) or water
¹/₂ tsp sesame oil
coriander (cilantro) leaves, to garnish

1 Cut the crab in half from the underbelly. Break off the claws and crack them with the back of the cleaver or a large kitchen knife.

2 Discard the legs and crack the shell, breaking it into several pieces. Discard the feathery gills and the stomach sac. Place in a bowl with the wine, egg and cornflour (cornstarch) and leave to marinate for 10–15 minutes.

3 Heat the oil in a preheated wok and stir-fry the crab with ginger and spring onions (scallions) for 2–3 minutes.

4 Add the soy sauce, sugar and stock or water, blend well and bring to the boil. Cover and cook for 3–4 minutes, then remove the cover, sprinkle with sesame oil and serve.

TECHNIQUES

The term 'baked' may be used on Chinese restaurant menus to describe dishes such as this one, which are actually cooked in a wok. 'Pot-roasted' may be a more accurate way to describe this cooking technique.

BUYING CRABS

Crabs are almost always sold ready-cooked. The crab should feel heavy for its size, and when it is shaken, there should be no sound of water inside. A good medium-sized crab should yield about 500 g/1 lb meat, enough for 3-4 people.

FISH WITH BLACK BEAN SAUCE

Any firm and delicate fish steaks such as salmon or turbot can be cooked by the same method.

SERVES 4–6

1 sea bass, trout or turbot, weighing about
   750g/1½ lb, cleaned
1 tsp salt
1 tbsp sesame oil
2–3 spring onions (scallions), cut in half
   lengthways
1 tbsp light soy sauce
1 tbsp Chinese rice wine or dry sherry
1 tbsp finely shredded ginger root
1 tbsp oil
2 tbsp crushed black bean sauce
2 finely shredded spring onions (scallions)
coriander (cilantro) leaves, to garnish
   (optional)
lemon slices, to garnish

1 Score both sides of the fish with diagonal cuts at 2.5cm/1 inch intervals. Rub both the inside and outside of the fish with salt and sesame oil.

2 Place the fish on top of the spring onions (scallions) on a heatproof platter. Blend the soy sauce and wine with the ginger shreds and pour evenly all over the fish.

3 Place the fish on the platter in a very hot steamer (or inside a wok on a rack), cover and steam vigorously over boiling water for 12–15 minutes or until the flesh flakes easily.

4 Heat the oil until hot, then blend in the black bean sauce. Remove the fish and place on a serving dish. Pour the hot black bean sauce over the whole length of the fish and place the shredded spring onions (scallions) on top. Serve garnished with coriander (cilantro) leaves and lemon slices.

FISH STEAKS

If using fish steaks, rub them with the salt and sesame oil, but do not score with a knife. The fish may require less cooking, depending on the thickness of the steaks – test for doneness with a skewer after about 8 minutes.

STEP 1

STEP 2

STEP 3

STEP 4

CHICKEN FU-YUNG

Strictly speaking, a fu-yung dish (the name means white lotus petals) should use egg whites only to create a very delicate texture. But most people associate fu-yung with an omelette in Chinese restaurants.

SERVES 4

175 g/6 oz chicken breast fillet, skinned
½ tsp salt
pepper
1 tsp rice wine or dry sherry
1 tbsp cornflour (cornstarch)
3 eggs, beaten
½ tsp finely chopped spring onions (scallions)
3 tbsp vegetable oil
125 g/4 oz green peas
1 tsp light soy sauce
salt
few drops sesame oil

1 Cut the chicken across the grain into very small, paper-thin slices, using the cleaver. Place the slices in a shallow dish, add the half teaspoon salt, pepper, wine and cornflour (cornstarch) and turn in the mixture until they are well coated.

2 Beat the eggs in a small bowl with a pinch of salt and the spring onions (scallions).

3 Heat oil in a preheated wok. Add chicken slices and stir-fry for about 1 minute, making sure that the slices are kept separated. Pour the beaten eggs over the chicken, and lightly scramble

until set. Do not stir too vigorously, or the mixture will break up in the oil. Stir the oil from the bottom of the wok so that the fu-yung rises to the surface.

4 Add the peas, salt and soy sauce and blend well. Sprinkle with sesame oil and serve.

VARIATION

If available, chicken *goujons* can be used for this dish: these are small, delicate strips of chicken which require no further cutting and are very tender.

LEMON CHICKEN

Lemon sauce is a Cantonese speciality, easily available in bottles from Oriental stores, or you can make your own.

SERVES 4

350 g/12 oz chicken breast fillets, skinned
1 tbsp rice wine or dry sherry
1 egg, beaten
4 tbsp plain (all-purpose) flour blended with
   2 tbsp water
vegetable oil for deep-frying
ready-made lemon sauce, or homemade
   sauce (see right)
salt and pepper
fresh lemon slices, to garnish

1 Cut the chicken into thin slices and place in a shallow dish with wine, salt and pepper. Leave to marinate for 25–30 minutes.

2 Make a batter with the egg and flour paste. Place the chicken slices in the batter and turn to coat well.

3 Heat the oil in a preheated wok or a deep-fryer. Deep-fry the chicken slices until golden brown, remove with a slotted spoon and drain on paper towels. Cut the chicken into bite-sized pieces.

4 Heat about 1 tablespoon oil in a preheated wok. Stir in the lemon sauce until well blended and pour over the chicken. Garnish with lemon slices.

LEMON SAUCE:
1 tbsp vegetable oil
250 ml/8 fl oz/1 cup Chinese Stock (see
   page 230)
1 tbsp caster sugar
1 tbsp lemon juice
1 tbsp cornflour (cornstarch)
1 tsp salt
1 tsp grated lemon rind

Heat the oil in a preheated wok until hot, reduce the heat and add all the other ingredients. Blend well, then bring to the boil and stir until smooth.

BOTTLED SAUCES

Many ready-made sauces are now available, and they are very useful if you are short of time. However, try to find time to make this homemade lemon sauce which has a delicious fresh taste.

STEP 1

STEP 2

STEP 3

STEP 4

CHICKEN WITH BEAN-SPROUTS

This is the basic Chicken Chop Suey to be found in almost every Chinese restaurant and takeaway (carry-out) all over the world.

SERVES 4

125 g/4 oz chicken breast fillet, skinned
1 tsp salt
¼ egg white, lightly beaten
2 tsp cornflour (cornstarch) paste (see page 231)
about 300 ml/½ pint/1 ¼ cups vegetable oil
1 small onion, thinly shredded
1 small green (bell) pepper, cored, deseeded and thinly shredded
1 small carrot, thinly shredded
125 g/4 oz/2 cups fresh bean-sprouts
½ tsp sugar
1 tbsp light soy sauce
1 tsp rice wine or dry sherry
2–3 tbsp Chinese Stock (see page 230)
a few drops sesame oil
chilli sauce, to serve

1 Thinly shred the chicken and mix with a pinch of the salt, the egg white and cornflour (cornstarch) paste.

2 Heat the oil in a preheated wok and stir-fry the chicken for about 1 minute, stirring to separate the shreds. Remove with a slotted spoon and drain on paper towels.

3 Pour off the oil, leaving about 2 tablespoons in the wok. Add all the vegetables except the bean-sprouts and stir-fry for about 2 minutes, then add the bean-sprouts and stir for a few seconds.

4 Return the chicken to the wok with the remaining salt, sugar, soy sauce and wine, blend well and add the stock or water. Sprinkle with the sesame oil and serve at once.

CHICKEN CHOP SUEY

Chop Suey actually originated in San Francisco at the turn of the century when Chinese immigrants were first settling there, and was first devised as a handy dish for using up leftovers.

STEP 1

STEP 2

STEP 3

STEP 4

CHICKEN WITH MUSHROOMS

*Dried Chinese mushrooms (shiitake) should be used for this dish –
otherwise use black rather than white fresh mushrooms.*

SERVES 4

*300–350 g/10–12 oz chicken, boned and
  skinned*
¹/₂ tsp sugar
1 tbsp light soy sauce
1 tsp rice wine or dry sherry
2 tsp cornflour (cornstarch)
*4–6 dried Chinese mushrooms, soaked in
  warm water*
1 tbsp finely shredded ginger root
salt and pepper
a few drops sesame oil
coriander (cilantro) leaves, to garnish

1 Cut the chicken into small bite-sized pieces and place in a bowl. Add the sugar, soy sauce, wine and cornflour (cornstarch) and leave to marinate for 25–30 minutes.

2 Drain the mushrooms and dry on paper towels. Slice the mushrooms into thin shreds, discarding any hard pieces of stalk (stem).

3 Place the chicken pieces on a heatproof dish that will fit inside a bamboo steamer. Arrange the mushroom and ginger shreds on top of the chicken and sprinkle with salt, pepper and sesame oil.

4 Place the dish on the rack inside a hot steamer or on a rack in a wok filled with hot water. Steam over high heat for 20 minutes. Serve hot, garnished with coriander (cilantro) leaves.

CHINESE MUSHROOMS

Chinese mushrooms come in many varieties: Shiitake are the best, and the two terms are often used synonymously. These fragrant mushrooms are most readily available at Oriental food stores and supermarkets but are also seasonally available.

Do not throw away the soaking water from the dried Chinese mushrooms. It is very useful, as it can be added to soups and stocks to give extra flavour.

STEP 1

STEP 2

STEP 3

STEP 4

DUCK WITH PINEAPPLE

For best results, use ready-cooked duck meat, widely available from Chinese restaurants and takeaways (carry-outs).

SERVES 4

125–175 g/4–6 oz cooked duck meat
3 tbsp vegetable oil
1 small onion, thinly shredded
2–3 slices ginger root, thinly shredded
1 spring onion (scallion), thinly shredded
1 small carrot, thinly shredded
125 g/4 oz canned pineapple, cut into small
slices
½ tsp salt
1 tbsp red rice vinegar
2 tbsp syrup from the pineapple
1 tbsp cornflour (cornstarch) paste (see page
231)
black bean sauce, to serve (optional)

1 Cut the cooked duck meat into thin strips.

2 Heat the oil in a preheated wok. Add the shredded onion and stir-fry until the shreds are opaque. Add the ginger, spring onion (scallion) and carrot shreds. Stir-fry for about 1 minute.

3 Add the duck shreds and pineapple to the wok together with the salt, rice vinegar and the pineapple syrup. Stir until the mixture is blended well.

4 Add the cornflour (cornstarch) paste and stir for 1–2 minutes until the sauce has thickened. Serve hot.

CANNED PINEAPPLE

Fortunately, most canned fruit is now available preserved in juice rather than syrup. The sugared syrup once used exclusively for this purpose was cloyingly sweet. To prepare this dish, be sure to choose pineapple in juice rather than syrup, so that the sauce is pleasantly tangy rather than overwhelmingly sugary.

STEP 1

STEP 2

STEP 3

STEP 4

STIR-FRIED PORK WITH VEGETABLES

This is a basic 'meat and veg' recipe – the meat can be pork, chicken, beef or lamb, and the vegetables can be varied according to seasonal availability.

SERVES 4

250 g/8 oz pork fillet (tenderloin), sliced
1 tsp sugar
1 tbsp light soy sauce
1 tsp rice wine or dry sherry
1 tsp cornflour (cornstarch) paste (see page 231)
1 small carrot
1 small green (bell) pepper, cored and deseeded
about 175 g/6 oz Chinese leaves
4 tbsp vegetable oil
1 spring onion (scallion), cut into short sections
a few small peeled ginger root slices
1 tsp salt
2–3 tbsp Chinese Stock (see page 230) or water
a few drops sesame oil

1 Thinly slice the pork fillet (tenderloin) into small pieces and place in a shallow dish. Add half the sugar and the soy sauce, the wine and cornflour (cornstarch) paste. Place in the refrigerator and marinate for 10–15 minutes.

2 Cut the carrot, green (bell) pepper and Chinese leaves into thin slices roughly the same length and width as the pork pieces so they cook in the same amount of time.

3 Heat the oil in a preheated wok. Stir-fry the pork for about 1 minute to seal in the flavour. Remove with a slotted spoon and keep warm.

4 Add the carrot, (bell) pepper, Chinese leaves, spring onion (scallion) and ginger and stir-fry for about 2 minutes.

5 Add the salt and remaining sugar, followed by the pork and remaining soy sauce, and the stock or water. Blend well and stir for another 1–2 minutes until hot. Sprinkle with the sesame oil and serve.

VARIATIONS

This dish can be made with other meats, as mentioned in the introduction. If using chicken strips, reduce the initial cooking time in the wok.

SWEET & SOUR PORK

This has to be the most popular Chinese dish all over the world.
The pork can be replaced with almost any other ingredient:
fish, prawns (shrimp), chicken or even vegetables.

STEP 1

STEP 2

STEP 3

STEP 4

SERVES 4

250–300 g/8–10 oz lean pork
2 tsp brandy or whisky
vegetable oil, for deep-frying
1 egg, beaten
2 tbsp plain (all-purpose) flour
salt and pepper

SAUCE:
1 tbsp vegetable oil
1 small onion, diced
1 small carrot, diced
¹/₂ small green (bell) pepper, cored, deseeded
    and diced
1 tbsp light soy sauce
3 tbsp sugar
3 tbsp wine vinegar
1 tbsp tomato purée (paste)
about 3–4 tbsp Chinese Stock (see page
    230) or water
1 tbsp cornflour (cornstarch) paste (see
    page 231)

1 Cut the pork into small bite-sized cubes. Place in a dish with the salt, pepper and brandy and leave to marinate for 15–20 minutes.

2 Heat the oil in a preheated wok or a deep-fryer. Place the pork cubes in a bowl with the beaten egg and stir to coat. Sprinkle on the flour and turn the pork cubes until they are well coated.

3 Deep-fry the pork cubes in batches for 3–4 minutes, stirring gently to separate the pieces. Remove with a slotted spoon or strainer and drain on paper towels. Reheat the oil until hot, and return the meat to the wok for another minute or so or until golden brown. Remove with a slotted spoon and drain on paper towels.

4 To make the sauce, heat the oil in a preheated wok or pan. Add the vegetables and stir-fry for about 1 minute. Add the seasonings and tomato purée (paste) with stock or water, bring to the boil and thicken with the cornflour (cornstarch) paste.

5 Add the pork and blend well so that each piece of meat is coated with the sauce. Serve hot.

SPARE RIBS WITH CHILLI

For best results, chop the spare ribs into small bite-size pieces.

STEP 1

SERVES 4

500 g/ 1 lb pork spare ribs
1 tsp sugar
1 tbsp light soy sauce
1 tsp rice wine or dry sherry
1 tsp cornflour (cornstarch)
about 600 ml/ 1pint/ 2 ½ cups vegetable oil
1 garlic clove, finely chopped
1 spring onion (scallion), cut into short
    sections
1 small hot chilli pepper (green or red),
    thinly sliced
2 tbsp black bean sauce
about 150 ml/¼ pint/⅔ cup Chinese Stock
    (see page 230) or water
1 small onion, diced
1 green (bell) pepper, cored, deseeded and
    diced

1 Trim excess fat from the ribs, and
chop each one into 3–4 bite-sized
pieces. Place the ribs in a shallow dish
with the sugar, soy sauce, wine and
cornflour (cornstarch) and leave to
marinate for 35–45 minutes.

2 Heat the oil in a preheated wok.
Add the spare ribs and deep-fry for
2–3 minutes until light brown. Remove
with a slotted spoon and drain well on
paper towels.

3 Pour off the oil, leaving about 1
tablespoon in the wok. Add the
garlic, spring onion (scallion), chilli
pepper and black bean sauce and stir-fry
for 30–40 seconds.

4 Add the spare ribs, blend well, then
add the stock or water. Bring to the
boil, then reduce the heat, cover and
braise for 8–10 minutes, stirring once or
twice.

5 Add the onion and green (bell)
pepper, increase the heat to high,
and stir uncovered for about 2 minutes to
reduce the sauce a little. Serve hot.

STEP 2

STEP 3

HANDLING CHILLIES

Be very careful when handling and cutting
chilli peppers as they exude a juice which
can cause irritation of the skin. Be sure to
wash your hands after handling, and keep
well away from face and eyes. It is the
seeds of the chilli that are the hottest part
– remove seeds if you do not want a very
hot dish.

STEP 5

STEP 1

STEP 2

STEP 3

STEP 4

OYSTER SAUCE BEEF

Like Stir-fried Pork with Vegetables (see page 54), the vegetables used in this recipe can be varied as you wish.

SERVES 4

300 g/10 oz beef steak
1 tsp sugar
1 tbsp light soy sauce
1 tsp rice wine or dry sherry
1 tsp cornflour (cornstarch) paste (see
    page 231)
½ small carrot
60 g/2 oz mangetout (snow peas)
60 g/2 oz canned bamboo shoots, rinsed and
    drained
60 g/2 oz canned straw mushrooms, rinsed
    and drained
about 300 ml/½ pint/1¼ cups vegetable oil
1 spring onion (scallion), cut into short
    sections
2–3 small slices ginger root
½ tsp salt
2 tbsp oyster sauce
2–3 tbsp Chinese Stock (see page 230)
    or water

1 Cut the beef into small, thin slices. Place in a shallow dish with the sugar, soy sauce, wine and cornflour (cornstarch) paste and leave to marinate for 25–30 minutes.

2 Slice the carrots, mangetout (snow peas), bamboo shoots and straw mushrooms so that as far as possible the

vegetable pieces are of uniform size and thickness so they cook in the same time.

3 Heat the oil in a preheated wok. Add the beef slices and stir-fry for about 1 minute, then remove with a slotted spoon and keep warm.

4 Pour off the oil, leaving about 1 tablespoon in the wok. Add the sliced vegetables with the spring onion (scallion) and ginger and stir-fry for about 2 minutes. Add the salt, beef and the oyster sauce with stock or water. Blend well until heated through, and serve with a dip sauce, if liked.

VARIATIONS

You can use whatever vegetables are available for this dish, but it is important to get a good contrast of colour – don't use all red or all green for example.

CHAPTER FOUR

Vegetables

Being basically an agricultural country, China has really perfected vegetable cooking into a fine art – almost all are cooked for a very short time, thus preserving their natural flavours and textures, as well as the vitamins and the brightness of their colours.

The Chinese eat far more vegetables than meat or poultry, and with a few exceptions, almost all meat and poultry dishes include some kind of vegetable as a supplementary ingredient – the idea being to give the dish a harmonious balance of colour, aroma, flavour and texture.

When selecting vegetables for cooking, the Chinese attach great importance to the freshness of ingredients used. Always buy crisp, firm vegetables, and cook them as soon as possible. Another point to remember is to wash the vegetables just before cutting, in order to avoid losing vitamins in water, and to cook them as soon as they have been cut so that the vitamin content is not lost through evaporation.

Opposite: *A stallholder in Mongolia proudly displays his selection of fruit and vegetables. Chinese cooks attach great importance to freshness, and visit the market daily to buy fresh produce for the family meal.*

STEP 1

STEP 2

STEP 3

STEP 4

STIR-FRIED MIXED VEGETABLES

The Chinese never mix ingredients indiscriminately – they are carefully selected to achieve a harmonious balance of contrasting colours and textures.

SERVES 4

60g/2 oz mangetout (snow peas)
1 small carrot
125 g/4 oz Chinese leaves
125 g/4 oz/2 cups fresh bean-sprouts
60 g/2 oz black or white mushrooms
60 g/2 oz canned bamboo shoots, rinsed
   and drained
3–4 tbsp vegetable oil
1 tsp salt
1 tsp sugar
1 tbsp oyster sauce or light soy sauce
a few drops sesame oil (optional)
dipping sauce, to serve (optional)

1 Prepare the vegetables: top and tail the mangetout (snow peas), and cut the carrot, Chinese leaves, mushrooms and bamboo shoots into roughly the same shape and size as the mangetout (snow peas).

2 Heat the oil in a preheated wok, and add the carrot first. Stir-fry for a few seconds, then add the mangetout (snow peas) and Chinese leaves and stir-fry for about 1 minute.

3 Add the bean-sprouts, mushrooms and bamboo shoots and stir-fry for another minute.

4 Add the salt and sugar, continue stirring for another minute, then add the oyster sauce or soy sauce, blend well, and sprinkle with sesame oil (if using). Serve hot or cold, with a dip sauce, if liked.

OYSTER SAUCE

This sauce, made from oysters cooked with salt and spices, is used in many Cantonese dishes. It is worth spending a little more on a good bottle of oyster sauce, as the more expensive brands are noticeably better. Good oyster sauce has a rich, almost beefy flavour. Once opened, a bottle of oyster sauce can be kept for months in the refrigerator and used to flavour a range of Oriental dishes.

BEAN-SPROUTS

It is important to use fresh bean-sprouts for this dish – the canned ones don't have the crunchy texture that is vital. If fresh ones are unavailable, select another vegetable, remembering to keep a colour contrast.

STEP 1

STEP 2

STEP 3

STEP 4

BROCCOLI IN OYSTER SAUCE

Some Cantonese restaurants use only the stalks (stems) of the broccoli for this dish, for the crunchy texture.

SERVES 4

250–300 g/8–10 oz broccoli
3 tbsp vegetable oil
3–4 small slices ginger root
1/2 tsp salt
1/2 tsp sugar
3–4 tbsp Chinese Stock (see page 230) or
  water
1 tbsp oyster sauce

1 Cut the broccoli spears into small florets. Trim the stalks (stems), peel off the rough skin, and cut the stalks (stems) diagonally into diamond-shaped chunks.

2 Heat the oil in a preheated wok and add the pieces of broccoli stalk (stem) and the ginger. Stir-fry for about 30 seconds, then add the broccoli florets and continue to stir-fry for another 2 minutes.

3 Add the salt, sugar and stock or water, and continue stirring for another minute or so.

4 Blend in the oyster sauce. Serve hot or leave until cold.

BROCCOLI STALKS (STEMS)

The broccoli stalks (stems) have to be peeled and cut diagonally to ensure they cook evenly. If they are thin, the pieces can be added to the wok at the same time as the florets, but otherwise add the stalks (stems) first, to ensure they will be tender.

VARIATION

Any crunchy-textured vegetable can be used in this recipe. If preferred, you could use cauliflower, celery, courgettes (zucchini), French (green) beans, etc., making sure that they are cut into even-sized pieces.

BRAISED CHINESE VEGETABLES

This dish is also known as Lo Han Zhai or Buddha's Delight. The original recipe calls for no less than 18 different vegetables to represent the 18 Buddhas (Lo Han) but six to eight are quite acceptable.

STEP 1

SERVES 4

5 g/¹⁄₄ oz dried wood ears
1 cake tofu (bean curd)
60 g/2 oz mangetout (snow peas)
125 g/4 oz Chinese leaves
1 small carrot
90 g/3 oz canned baby corn, drained
90 g/3 oz canned straw mushrooms, rinsed
   and drained
60 g/2 oz canned water chestnuts, rinsed
   and drained
300 ml/¹⁄₂ pint/1¹⁄₄ cups vegetable oil
1 tsp salt
¹⁄₂ tsp sugar
1 tbsp light soy sauce or oyster sauce
2–3 tbsp Chinese Stock (see page 230) or
   water
a few drops sesame oil

1 Soak the wood ears in warm water for 15–20 minutes, then rinse and drain, discarding any hard bits. Dry on paper towels.

2 Cut the cake of tofu (bean curd) into about 18 small pieces. Top and tail the mangetout (snow peas). Cut the Chinese leaves and the carrot into slices roughly the same size and shape as the mangetout (snow peas). Cut the baby

STEP 2

corn, the straw mushrooms and the water chestnuts in half.

3 Heat the oil in a preheated wok. Add the tofu (bean curd) and deep-fry for about 2 minutes until it turns slightly golden. Remove with a slotted spoon and drain on paper towels.

4 Pour off the oil, leaving about 2 tablespoons in the wok. Add the carrot, Chinese leaves and mangetout (snow peas) and stir-fry for about 1 minute.

5 Add the baby corn, mushrooms and water chestnuts. Stir gently for 2 more minutes, then add the salt, sugar, soy sauce and stock or water. Bring to the boil and stir-fry for 1 more minute.

6 Sprinkle with sesame oil and serve hot or cold.

STEP 3

WOOD EARS

Wood ears (a kind of fungus) can usually be obtained in Chinese supermarkets. If unavailable, use another variety of Chinese mushrooms.

STEP 5

STEP 1

STEP 2

STEP 3

STEP 4

STIR-FRIED BEAN-SPROUTS

Be sure to use fresh bean-sprouts, rather than the canned variety, for this crunchy-textured dish.

SERVES 4

250 g/8 oz/4 cups fresh bean-sprouts
2–3 spring onions (scallions)
1 red chilli pepper (optional)
3 tbsp vegetable oil
½ tsp salt
½ tsp sugar
1 tbsp light soy sauce
a few drops sesame oil (optional)

1 Rinse the bean-sprouts in cold water, discarding any husks or small pieces that float to the top. Drain well on paper towels.

2 Cut the spring onions (scallions) into short sections. Thinly shred the red chilli pepper, if using, discarding the seeds.

3 Heat the oil in a preheated wok. Add the bean-sprouts, spring onions (scallions) and chilli pepper, if using, and stir-fry for about 2 minutes.

4 Add the salt, sugar, soy sauce and sesame oil, if using, to the mixture in the wok. Stir well to blend. Serve hot or cold.

TO GROW BEAN-SPROUTS

It is very easy to grow bean-sprouts. If you find it difficult to buy fresh ones, this could be the answer. Use dried mung beans, obtainable from supermarkets and health-food stores. Wash the beans thoroughly in several changes of water. Place in a lidded jar, or a seed sprouter if you have one, and place in a warm, dark place (an airing cupboard is ideal). Check daily and rinse with a little water to keep them moist. You should have sprouts that are ready to use in 3–4 days.

VARIATION

The red chilli pepper gives a bite to this dish – leave the seeds in for an even hotter taste. If you prefer a milder, sweeter flavour, use red (bell) pepper instead of the chilli pepper. Core, seed and cut into strips in the same way.

CHAPTER FIVE

Rice & Noodles

Rice and noodles provide bulk in the Chinese diet, but the recipes given here are meant to be served on their own, as a light meal or as a snack. For an everyday meal, plain rice is served with two or three other dishes – usually meat and vegetables together with a soup. Fried rice and chow mein are only served at formal occasions, or as a snack between main meals.

In China, noodles are always served at birthday celebrations, as the Chinese consider that the length of noodles symbolizes long life.

The Chinese do not normally conclude an everyday meal with a dessert, but fresh fruit can always be served for those who are used to finishing off a meal with something sweet.

Opposite: *A woman tends the irrigation system in rice paddy fields near Guilin. Rice is the most important staple in the Chinese diet, and vast tracts of fertile land are given over to its cultivation.*

STEP 1

STEP 3

STEP 3

STEP 5

SEAFOOD CHOW MEIN

Use whatever seafood is available for this delicious noodle dish –
mussels or crab would also be suitable. Simply add to the wok with
the other seafood in step 6.

SERVES 4

90 g/3 oz squid, cleaned (see page 36)
3–4 fresh scallops
90 g/3 oz raw prawns (shrimp), peeled
½ egg white, lightly beaten
1 tbsp cornflour (cornstarch) paste (see page
* 231)*
275 g/9 oz Chinese egg noodles
5–6 tbsp vegetable oil
2 tbsp light soy sauce
60 g/2 oz mangetout (snow peas)
½ tsp salt
½ tsp sugar
1 tsp Chinese rice wine or dry sherry
2 spring onions (scallions), finely shredded
a few drops sesame oil

1 Open up the squid and score the
inside in a criss-cross pattern, then
cut into pieces, each about the size of a
postage stamp.

2 Soak the squid in a bowl of boiling
water until all the pieces curl up.
Rinse in cold water and drain.

3 Cut each scallop into 3–4 slices.
Cut the prawns (shrimp) in half
lengthways if large. Mix the scallops and
prawns with the egg white and cornflour
(cornstarch) paste.

4 Cook the noodles in boiling water
according to the instructions on
the packet, then drain and rinse under
cold water. Drain well, then toss with
about 1 tablespoon of oil.

5 Heat 3 tablespoons oil in a
preheated wok. Add the noodles
and 1 tablespoon of the soy sauce and
stir-fry for 2–3 minutes. Remove to a
large serving dish.

6 Heat the remaining oil in the wok
and add the mangetout (snow
peas) and seafood. Stir-fry for about 2
minutes, then add the salt, sugar, wine,
remaining soy sauce and about half the
spring onions (scallions). Blend well and
add a little stock or water if necessary.

7 Pour the seafood mixture on top of
the noodles and sprinkle with
sesame oil. Garnish with the remaining
spring onions (scallions) and serve hot or
at room temperature.

STEP 1

FRIED NOODLES (CHOW MEIN)

This is a basic recipe for Chow Mein. Additional ingredients such as vegetables (see page 144), chicken or pork (see page 220) or seafood (see page 74) can be added if liked.

STEP 2

SERVES 4

275 g/9 oz Chinese egg noodles
3–4 tbsp vegetable oil
1 small onion, finely shredded
125 g/4 oz/2 cups fresh bean-sprouts
1 spring onion (scallion), finely shredded
2 tbsp light soy sauce
a few drops sesame oil

1 Cook the noodles in salted boiling water according to the instructions on the packet (usually no more than 4–5 minutes).

2 Drain and rinse the noodles in cold water; drain well, then toss with a little vegetable oil.

STEP 3

3 Heat the remaining oil in a preheated wok. Stir-fry the onion for about 30–40 seconds, then add the bean-sprouts and noodles, stir and toss for 1 more minute.

FRESH NOODLES

Chinese egg noodles are made from wheat or rice flour, water and egg. Handmade noodles are made by an elaborate process of kneading, pulling and twisting the dough, and it takes years to learn the art. Noodles are a symbol of longevity, and so are always served at birthday celebrations – it is regarded as bad luck to cut them. If fresh egg noodles are available, these require very little cooking: simply place in boiling water for about 3 minutes, then drain and toss in oil. Noodles can be boiled and eaten plain, or stir-fried with meat and vegetables for a light meal or snack.

4 Add the spring onion (scallion) and soy sauce and blend well. Sprinkle with the sesame oil and serve.

STEP 4

STEP 1

STEP 2

STEP 3

STEP 4

SINGAPORE-STYLE RICE NOODLES

Rice noodles or vermicelli are also known as rice sticks. Egg noodles can also be used for this dish, but it will not taste the same. The ideal meat to use is Barbecue Pork (see page 22).

SERVES 4

200 g/7 oz rice vermicelli
125 g/4 oz cooked chicken or pork
60 g/2 oz peeled prawns (shrimp), defrosted
   if frozen
4 tbsp vegetable oil
1 onion, thinly shredded
125 g/4 oz/2 cups fresh bean-sprouts
1 tsp salt
1 tbsp mild curry powder
2 tbsp light soy sauce
2 spring onions (scallions), thinly shredded
1–2 small fresh green or red chilli peppers,
   deseeded and thinly shredded

1 Soak the rice vermicelli in boiling water for 8–10 minutes, then rinse in cold water and drain well.

2 Thinly slice the cooked meat. Dry the prawns (shrimp) thoroughly on paper towels.

3 Heat the oil in a preheated wok. Add the onion and stir-fry until opaque. Add the bean-sprouts and stir-fry for 1 minute.

4 Add the noodles with the meat and prawns (shrimp), and continue stirring for another minute.

5 Blend in the salt, curry powder and soy sauce, followed by the spring onions (scallions) and chilli peppers. Stir-fry for 1 more minute, then serve at once.

RICE NOODLES

Rice noodles are very delicate noodles made from rice flour. They become soft and pliable after being soaked for about 15 minutes. If you wish to store them after they have been soaked, toss them in a few drops of sesame oil, then place them in a sealed container in the refrigerator.

VARIATION

For a really authentic flavour include 1 tablespoon dried shrimps, which have a strong, pungent taste. Soak them in warm water for 30 minutes, drain and add to the noodles in step 4.

SPECIAL FRIED RICE

Special Fried Rice, sometimes called Yangchow Fried Rice, is almost a meal in itself. Make sure the cooked rice is completely dry and cold before adding it to the wok, otherwise it might stick and become lumpy.

STEP 1

STEP 2

SERVES 4

60 g/2 oz peeled prawns (shrimp)
60 g/2 oz cooked meat (chicken, pork or
    ham)
125 g/4 oz green peas
3 eggs
1 tsp salt
2 spring onions (scallions), finely chopped
4 tbsp vegetable oil
1 tbsp light soy sauce
1 tsp Chinese rice wine or dry sherry
    (optional)
500 g/1 lb/4 cups cooked rice

1 Dry the prawns (shrimp) on paper towels. Cut the meat into small dice about the same size as the peas.

2 In a bowl, lightly beat the eggs with a pinch of salt and a few pieces of the spring onions (scallions).

3 Heat 2 tablespoons of the oil in a preheated wok. Add the peas, prawns (shrimp) and meat and stir-fry for about 1 minute. Stir in the soy sauce and wine, then remove and keep warm.

4 Heat the remaining oil and add the eggs. Stir to lightly scramble. Add the rice and stir to separate the grains,

then add the remaining salt and spring onions (scallions), and the prawns (shrimp), meat and peas. Blend well and serve hot or cold.

STEP 3

STEP 4

FRESH PEAS

Fresh peas straight from the shell really do make a difference to this dish. Their vivid, emerald colour and just-off-the-vine flavour make it worth the (relatively small) amount of effort. Shell and lightly blanch the peas before stir-frying them.

PERFECT RICE

Cook the rice by the absorption method as described on page 232. Leave to stand, covered, until the rice has absorbed all the water, then turn out on to a large flat plate or baking sheet (cookie sheet). Spread the rice out and leave until completely cold and dry.

APPETIZERS

•

SOUPS

•

MAIN MEALS

•

VEGETABLES & SALADS

•

RICE & NOODLES

2

VEGETARIAN CHINESE COOKING

CHAPTER SIX

Appetizers

A selection of small portions of several different dishes usually starts the Chinese meal. The majority of these appetizers consist of tasty fillings enclosed in pastry-type wrappers which are fried until crisp. These are served with a simple dipping sauce of soy sauce, sherry and strips of spring onion (scallion) and chilli.

Snacks and appetizers are also sold at many roadside stalls throughout China, and are bought and eaten by people as they go about their daily tasks. After dusk, the pavements are filled with groups of families and friends cooking, eating and selling many delicious meals; this is an important part of their social lives, and is an enjoyable way of getting together and sharing their food.

Use the dishes in this section as appetizers to the main meal, or as snacks in their own right.

Opposite: *Hong Kong harbour shrouded in mist.*

STEP 1

STEP 2

STEP 3

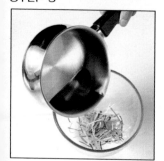

STEP 4

CRISPY WONTONS WITH PIQUANT DIPPING SAUCE

Mushroom-filled crispy wontons are served on skewers with a dipping sauce flavoured with chillies.

SERVES 4

1 tbsp vegetable oil
1 tbsp chopped onion
1 small garlic clove, chopped
$1/2$ tsp chopped ginger root
60 g/2 oz/$1/2$ cup flat mushrooms, chopped
16 wonton skins (see page 100)
vegetable oil for deep-frying
salt
8 wooden skewers

SAUCE:
2 tbsp vegetable oil
2 spring onions (scallions), thinly shredded
1 red and 1 green chilli, deseeded and thinly
   shredded
3 tbsp light soy sauce
1 tbsp vinegar
1 tbsp dry sherry
pinch sugar

1 Heat the oil in a preheated wok or frying pan (skillet). Add the onion, garlic and ginger root, and stir-fry for 2 minutes. Stir in the mushrooms and fry for a further 2 minutes. Season well with salt and leave to cool.

2 Place 1 teaspoon of the cooled mushroom filling in the centre of each wonton skin. Bring 2 opposite corners together to cover the mixture and pinch together to seal. Repeat with the remaining corners.

3 Thread 2 wontons on to each skewer. Heat enough oil in a large saucepan to deep-fry the wontons in batches until golden and crisp. Remove with a perforated spoon and drain on paper towels.

4 To make the sauce, heat the oil in a small saucepan until quite hot and a small cube of bread dropped in the oil browns in a few seconds. Put the spring onions (scallions) and chillies in a bowl and pour the hot oil slowly on top. Then mix in the remaining ingredients and serve with the crispy wontons.

HEATING THE OIL

Do not overheat the oil for deep-frying, or the wontons will brown on the outside before they are properly cooked inside.

STEP 2

STEP 3

STEP 4

STEP 5

CRISPY SEAWEED

Popular in many Chinese restaurants, this dish is served as a first course. This 'seaweed' is, in fact, deep-fried spring greens.

SERVES 4

250 g/8 oz spring greens
vegetable oil for deep-frying
1½ tsp caster (superfine) sugar
1 tsp salt
30 g/1 oz/¼ cup flaked (slivered) almonds

1 Wash the spring greens thoroughly. Trim off the excess tough stalks (stems). Place on paper towels or a dry tea towel (dish cloth) and leave to drain thoroughly.

2 Using a sharp knife, shred the spring greens finely and spread out on several layers of paper towels for about 30 minutes to dry.

3 Heat the oil in a preheated wok or a deep-fryer. Remove the pan from the heat and add the spring greens in batches. Return the pan to the heat and deep-fry until the greens begin to float to the surface and become translucent and crinkled. Remove the spring greens, using a perforated spoon, and drain on paper towels. Keep each batch warm.

4 Mix the sugar and salt together, sprinkle over the 'seaweed' and toss together to mix well.

5 Add the flaked (slivered) almonds to the hot oil and fry until lightly golden. Remove with a perforated spoon and drain on paper towels.

6 Serve the crispy 'seaweed' with the flaked (slivered) almonds.

TIME-SAVER

As a time-saver you can use a food processor to shred the greens finely. Make sure you use only the best of the leaves; sort through the spring greens and discard any tough outer leaves, as these will spoil the overall taste and texture if they are included.

STEP 2

TOFU (BEAN CURD) SANDWICHES

Slices of tofu (bean curd) are sandwiched together with a cucumber and cream cheese filling and coated in batter. Serve with a mint and yogurt dipping sauce.

MAKES 28

4 Chinese dried mushrooms (if unavailable,
　use thinly sliced open-cup mushrooms)
275 g/9 oz tofu (bean curd)
½ cucumber, grated
1 cm/½ inch piece ginger root, grated
60 g/2 oz/¼ cup cream cheese
salt and pepper

BATTER:
125 g/4 oz/1 cup plain (all-purpose)
　flour
1 egg, beaten
120 ml/4 fl oz/½ cup water
½ tsp salt
2 tbsp sesame seeds
vegetable oil for deep-frying

SAUCE:
150 ml/¼ pint/⅔ cup natural yogurt
2 tsp honey
2 tbsp chopped fresh mint

1 Place the mushrooms in a small bowl and cover with warm water. Leave to soak for 20–25 minutes. Drain and squeeze out the excess water. Remove the tough centres and chop the mushrooms.

2 Drain the tofu (bean curd) and slice thinly. Then cut each slice to make 2.5 cm/1 inch squares.

3 Squeeze the excess liquid from the cucumber and mix the cucumber with the mushrooms, grated ginger and cream cheese. Season well. Use as a filling to sandwich slices of tofu (bean curd) together to make about 28 sandwiches.

4 To make the batter, sift the flour into a bowl. Beat in the egg, water and salt to make a thick batter. Stir in the sesame seeds. Heat the oil in a large preheated wok or saucepan. Coat the sandwiches in the batter and deep-fry in batches until golden. Remove with a slotted spoon and drain on paper towels.

5 To make the dipping sauce, blend together the yogurt, honey and mint. Serve with the tofu (bean curd) sandwiches.

VARIATION

For a change you could try using smoked tofu (bean curd), which will add extra flavour to the sandwiches.

STEP 3

STEP 4

STEP 5

STEP 2

STEP 3

STEP 4

STEP 5

SPRING (EGG) ROLLS

Thin slices of vegetables are wrapped in pastry and deep-fried until crisp. Spring (egg) roll wrappers are available fresh or frozen from Oriental suppliers and some supermarkets.

MAKES 12

5 Chinese dried mushrooms (if unavailable, use open-cup mushrooms)
1 large carrot
60 g/2 oz/1 cup canned bamboo shoots, rinsed and drained
2 spring onions (scallions)
60 g/2 oz Chinese leaves
2 tbsp vegetable oil
250 g/8 oz/4 cups bean-sprouts
1 tbsp soy sauce
12 spring (egg) roll wrappers
1 egg, beaten
vegetable oil for deep-frying
salt

1 Place the mushrooms in a small bowl and cover with warm water. Leave to soak for 20–25 minutes.

2 Drain the mushrooms and squeeze out the excess water. Remove the tough centres and slice the mushrooms thinly. Cut the carrot and bamboo shoots into very thin julienne strips. Chop the spring onions (scallions) and shred the Chinese leaves.

3 Heat the 2 tablespoons of oil in a preheated wok or frying pan (skillet). Add the mushrooms, carrot and bamboo shoots, continue stir-frying for about 2 minutes. Add the spring onions (scallions), Chinese leaves, bean-sprouts and soy sauce. Season with salt and stir-fry for 2 minutes. Leave to cool.

4 Divide the mixture into 12 equal portions and place one portion on the edge of each spring (egg) roll wrapper. Fold in the sides and roll each one up, brushing the join with a little beaten egg to seal.

5 Deep-fry the spring (egg) rolls in batches in hot oil in a wok or large saucepan for 4–5 minutes, or until golden and crispy. Take care that the oil is not too hot or the spring (egg) rolls will brown on the outside before cooking on the inside. Remove and drain on paper towels. Keep each batch warm while the others are being cooked. Serve at once.

SPRING (EGG) ROLL WRAPPERS

If spring (egg) roll wrappers are unavailable, use sheets of filo pastry instead.

SWEET & SOUR CUCUMBER

Chunks of cucumber are marinated in vinegar and sweetened with honey to make a sweet and sour appetizer.

STEP 1

STEP 2

STEP 3

STEP 4

SERVES 4

1 cucumber
1 tsp salt
2 tsp honey
2 tbsp rice vinegar
3 tbsp chopped fresh coriander (cilantro)
2 tsp sesame oil
1/4 tsp crushed red peppercorns
strips of red and yellow (bell) pepper, to
   garnish

1 Peel thin strips off the cucumber along the length. This gives a pretty striped effect. Cut the cucumber in quarters lengthways and then into 2.5 cm/1 inch long pieces. Place in a colander.

2 Sprinkle the salt over the cucumber and leave to rest for 30 minutes to allow the salt to draw out the excess water from the cucumber. Wash the cucumber thoroughly to remove the salt, drain and pat dry with paper towels.

3 Place the cucumber in a bowl. Combine the honey with the vinegar and pour over. Mix together and leave to marinate for 15 minutes.

4 Stir in the coriander (cilantro) and sesame oil, and place in a serving bowl.

5 Sprinkle over the crushed red peppercorns. Serve garnished with strips of red and yellow (bell) peppers.

RICE VINEGAR

Rice vinegar is a common Chinese cooking ingredient. White rice vinegar is made from rice wine, whereas red rice vinegar is made from fermented rice. Both have a distinctive flavour, but the white version tends to be used more often, as it will flavour but not colour all kinds of food. If rice vinegar is unavailable, use white wine vinegar instead.

CHAPTER SEVEN

Soups

In China soups are not usually served at the beginning of a meal but between courses to clear the palate. It is also quite common for Chinese families to have a large tureen of clear soup on the table which is served at the same time as the other dishes. Chinese cooks will often add some boiling clear stock or water to leftovers from the main course and serve it as an instant soup at the end of the meal.

Generally the soups are made from a good stock of vegetables, which are boiled for about 30 minutes before being strained, which gives a thin, clear broth. This can be served on its own, with a little soy sauce added for flavour. With the addition of a few suitable vegetables you can make a simple but tasty soup.

Most Chinese soups are of the thin, clear variety; however they do have a few thickened ones, such as the Hot & Sour Soup to which cornflour (cornstarch) is added. These soups can be eaten as a lunch or snack on their own.

Opposite: The familiar sight of a one-man 'taxi' in the back streets of Hong Kong.

STEP 1

STEP 2

STEP 3

STEP 4

VEGETARIAN HOT & SOUR SOUP

This is a popular Chinese soup, which is unusual in that it is thickened. The characteristic 'hot' flavour is achieved by the addition of plenty of black pepper.

SERVES 4

4 Chinese dried mushrooms (if unavailable,
  use open-cup mushrooms)
125 g/4 oz firm tofu (bean curd)
60 g/2 oz/1 cup canned bamboo shoots,
  rinsed and drained
600 ml/1 pint/2½ cups vegetable stock or
  water
60 g/2 oz/⅓ cup shelled peas
1 tbsp dark soy sauce
2 tbsp white wine vinegar
2 tbsp cornflour (cornstarch)
salt and pepper
sesame oil, to serve

1 Place the Chinese dried mushrooms in a small bowl and cover with warm water. Leave to soak for 20–25 minutes.

2 Drain the mushrooms and squeeze out the excess water, reserving it. Remove the tough centres and cut the mushrooms into thin shreds. Shred the tofu (bean curd) and bamboo shoots.

3 Bring the stock or water to the boil in a large saucepan. Add the mushrooms, tofu (bean curd), bamboo shoots and peas. Simmer for 2 minutes.

4 Mix together the soy sauce, vinegar and cornflour (cornstarch) with 2 tablespoons of the reserved mushroom liquid. Stir into the soup with the remaining mushroom liquid. Bring to the boil and season with salt and plenty of pepper. Simmer for 2 minutes.

5 Serve in warmed bowls with a few drops of sesame oil in each.

MUSHROOMS

If you use open-cup mushrooms instead of dried mushrooms, add an extra 150 ml/¼ pint/⅔ cup vegetable stock or water to the soup, as these mushrooms do not need soaking.

STEP 1

STEP 2

STEP 3

STEP 4

WONTON SOUP

*Spinach and pine kernel (nut) filled wontons are served in a clear soup.
The recipe for the wonton skins makes 24 but the soup requires only
half this quantity. The other half can be frozen ready for another time.*

SERVES 4

WONTON SKINS:
1 egg
6 tbsp water
250 g/ 8 oz/ 2 cups plain (all-purpose)
   flour

FILLING:
125 g/ 4 oz/ ¹/₂ cup frozen chopped spinach,
   defrosted
15 g/¹/₂ oz/ 1 tbsp pine kernels (nuts),
   toasted and chopped
30 g/ 1 oz/ ¹/₄ cup minced (ground) quorn
   (TVP)
salt

SOUP:
600 ml/ 1 pint/ 2¹/₂ cups vegetable stock
1 tbsp dry sherry
1 tbsp light soy sauce
2 spring onions (scallions), chopped

1 Beat the egg lightly in a bowl and
mix with the water. Stir in the flour
to form a stiff dough. Knead lightly, then
cover with a damp cloth and leave to rest
for 30 minutes.

2 Roll out the dough into a large
sheet about 5 mm/¹/₄ inch thick.
Cut out twenty-four 7 cm/3 inch

squares. Dust each one lightly with flour.
Only 12 squares are required for the soup
so freeze the remainder (see below).

3 To make the filling, squeeze out the
excess water from the spinach. Mix
the spinach with the pine kernels (nuts)
and quorn (TVP). Season with salt.

4 Divide the mixture into 12 equal
portions and place one portion in
the centre of each wonton square. Seal
by bringing the opposite corners of each
square together and squeezing well.

5 To make the soup, bring the stock,
sherry and soy sauce to the boil.
Add the wontons and boil rapidly for 2–3
minutes. Add the spring onions
(scallions) and serve in warmed bowls
immediately.

FREEZING WONTON
SKINS

To freeze the leftover wonton skins, place
small squares of baking parchment in
between each skin, then place in a freezer
bag and freeze. Defrost thoroughly before
using.

SWEETCORN (CORN) & LENTIL SOUP

This pale-coloured soup is made with sweetcorn (corn) and green lentils, and is similar in style to the traditional crab and sweetcorn (corn) soup on page 27.

SERVES 4

30 g/ 1 oz/ 2 tbsp green lentils
1 litre/ 1³/₄ pints/ 4 cups vegetable stock
1cm/¹/₂ inch piece ginger root, finely
  chopped
2 tsp soy sauce
1 tsp sugar
1 tbsp cornflour (cornstarch)
3 tbsp dry sherry
325 g/ 11 oz can sweetcorn (corn)
1 egg white
1 tsp sesame oil
salt and pepper

TO GARNISH:
strips spring onion (scallion)
strips red chilli

1 Wash the lentils in a sieve (strainer). Place in a saucepan with the stock, ginger root, soy sauce and sugar. Bring to the boil and boil rapidly, uncovered, for 10 minutes. Skim off any froth on the surface. Reduce the heat, cover and simmer for 15 minutes.

2 Mix the cornflour (cornstarch) with the sherry in a small bowl. Add the sweetcorn (corn) with the liquid from the can and cornflour (cornstarch) mixture to the saucepan. Simmer over a low heat for 2 minutes, stirring occasionally.

3 Whisk the egg white lightly with the sesame oil. Pour the egg mixture into the soup in a thin stream, remove from the heat and stir. The egg white will form white strands.

4 Season to taste. Pour into 4 warmed soup bowls and garnish with strips of spring onion (scallion) and chilli before serving.

USING CANNED LENTILS

As a time-saver use a 425 g/14 oz can of green lentils instead of dried ones. Place the lentils and sweetcorn (corn) together in a large saucepan with the stock and flavourings, bring to the boil and simmer for 2 minutes, then continue the recipe from step 2. There is no need to boil canned lentils rapidly for 10 minutes.

STEP 1

STEP 2

STEP 3

STEP 3

STEP 1

STEP 3

STEP 4

STEP 5

MUSHROOM & CUCUMBER NOODLE SOUP

A light, refreshing clear soup of mushrooms, cucumber and small pieces of rice noodles, flavoured with soy sauce and a touch of garlic.

SERVES 4

125 g/4 oz flat or open-cup mushrooms
1/2 cucumber
2 spring onions (scallions)
1 garlic clove
2 tbsp vegetable oil
30 g/1 oz/1/4 cup Chinese rice noodles
3/4 tsp salt
1 tbsp soy sauce

1 Wash the mushrooms and slice them thinly. Do not remove the peel as this adds more flavour. Halve the cucumber lengthways. Scoop out the seeds, using a teaspoon, and slice the cucumber thinly.

2 Chop the spring onions (scallions) finely and cut the garlic clove into thin strips.

3 Heat the oil in a preheated wok or large saucepan. Add the spring onions (scallions) and garlic, and stir-fry for 30 seconds. Add the mushrooms and stir-fry for 2–3 minutes.

4 Stir in 600 ml/1 pint/2 1/2 cups water. Break the noodles into short lengths and add to the soup. Bring to the boil over a high heat.

5 Add the cucumber slices, salt and soy sauce, stirring cccasionally.

6 Serve the soup in warmed bowls, distributing the noodles and vegetables evenly.

CUCUMBER SEEDS

Scooping the seeds out from the cucumber gives it a prettier effect when sliced, and also helps to reduce any bitterness, but if you prefer, you can leave them in.

STEP 1

STEP 2

STEP 3

STEP 4

LETTUCE & TOFU (BEAN CURD) SOUP

This is a delicate, clear soup of shredded lettuce and small chunks of tofu (bean curd) with sliced carrot and spring onion (scallion).

SERVES 4

200 g/7 oz tofu (bean curd)
2 tbsp vegetable oil
1 carrot, sliced thinly
1 cm/½ inch piece ginger root, cut into thin
  shreds
3 spring onions (scallions), sliced diagonally
1.25 litres/2 pints/5 cups vegetable stock
2 tbsp soy sauce
2 tbsp dry sherry
1 tsp sugar
125 g/4 oz/1½ cups cos (romaine) lettuce,
  shredded
salt and pepper

1 Cut the tofu (bean curd) into small cubes. Heat the oil in a preheated wok or large saucepan. Add the tofu (bean curd) and stir-fry until browned. Remove with a perforated spoon and drain on paper towels.

2 Add the carrot, ginger root and spring onions (scallions) to the wok or saucepan and stir-fry for 2 minutes.

3 Add the stock, soy sauce, sherry and sugar. Bring to the boil and simmer for 1 minute.

4 Add the lettuce and stir until it has just wilted.

5 Return the tofu (bean curd) to the pan to reheat. Season with salt and pepper and serve in warmed bowls.

DECORATIVE CARROTS

For a prettier effect, score grooves along the length of the carrot with a sharp knife before slicing. This will create a flower effect as the carrot is cut into rounds. You could also try slicing the carrot on the diagonal to make longer slices. Try garnishing the soup with carrot curls – very fine strips of carrot that have been placed in iced water to make them curl up.

CHAPTER EIGHT

Main Meals

An abundance of high-quality produce can be bought from the markets in the towns and villages of China, and fresh food is purchased daily by endless streams of people buying the freshest goods for their family meals.

The simplest meal has a central dish of rice or noodles with a stir-fry or steamed dumplings, all of which are served at the same time, quite different from our Western way of eating. When entertaining, choose several different dishes to give as much variety of taste as possible, and prepare as much as you can in advance to enable you to spend more time with your guests than in the kitchen.

The following recipes contain ingredients that blend together to achieve a balanced contrast in colour, flavour and texture. They are quick to prepare and cook. All the recipes in this section may be served as main courses with an accompaniment of rice or noodles.

Opposite: *One of the wonders of the world – the Great Wall of China.*

VEGETABLE & NUT STIR-FRY

*A colourful selection of vegetables are stir-fried in a creamy peanut
sauce and sprinkled with nuts to serve.*

STEP 1

STEP 3

STEP 4

STEP 5

SERVES 4

3 tbsp crunchy peanut butter
150 ml/^{1}/$_4$ pint/^{2}/$_3$ cup water
1 tbsp soy sauce
1 tsp sugar
1 carrot
^{1}/$_2$ red onion
4 baby courgettes (zucchini)
1 red (bell) pepper
250 g/8 oz Chinese egg noodles
30 g/1 oz/^{1}/$_4$ cup peanuts, roughly chopped
2 tbsp vegetable oil
1 tsp sesame oil
1 small green chilli, deseeded and thinly
    sliced
1 garlic clove, thinly sliced
225 g/7^1/$_2$ oz can water chestnuts, rinsed,
    drained and sliced
175 g/6 oz/3 cups bean-sprouts
salt

1 Blend the peanut butter with the
water gradually in a small bowl.
Stir in the soy sauce and sugar.

2 Cut the carrot into thin
matchsticks and slice the onion.
Slice the courgettes (zucchini) on the
diagonal and cut the (bell) pepper into
even chunks.

3 Bring a large pan of water to the
boil and add the egg noodles.
Remove from the heat immediately and
leave to rest for 4 minutes, stirring
occasionally to divide the noodles.

4 Heat a preheated wok or large
frying pan (skillet). Add the
peanuts and dry-fry until they are
beginning to brown. Remove and set aside.

5 Add the oils to the pan and heat.
Add the carrot, onion, courgette
(zucchini), (bell) pepper, chilli and garlic,
and stir-fry for 2–3 minutes. Add the
water chestnuts, bean-sprouts and
peanut sauce. Bring to the boil and heat
thoroughly. Season to taste. Drain the
noodles and serve with the stir-fry.
Sprinkle with the peanuts.

VARIATION

The vegetables in this dish can be varied
according to your taste and their
availability. Make sure you choose a
variety of colours for the best effect.

STEP 1

STEP 2

STEP 3

STEP 4

AUBERGINES (EGGPLANTS) IN BLACK BEAN SAUCE

Stir-fried aubergines (eggplants) are served in a black bean sauce with garlic and spring onions (scallions). This would go well with rice and another vegetable dish such as stir-fried baby corn and green beans.

SERVES 4

60 g/2 oz/generous ⅓ cup dried black beans
450 ml/¾ pint/scant 2 cups vegetable
 stock
1 tbsp malt vinegar
1 tbsp dry sherry
1 tbsp soy sauce
1 tbsp sugar
1½ tsp cornflour (cornstarch)
1 red chilli, deseeded and chopped
1 cm/½ inch piece ginger root, chopped
2 aubergines (eggplants)
2 tsp salt
3 tbsp vegetable oil
2 garlic cloves, sliced
4 spring onions (scallions), cut diagonally
shredded radishes, to garnish

1 Soak the beans overnight in plenty of cold water. Drain and place in a saucepan. Cover with cold water, bring to the boil and boil rapidly, uncovered, for 10 minutes. Drain. Return the beans to the saucepan with the stock and bring to the boil.

2 Blend together the vinegar, sherry, soy sauce, sugar, cornflour (cornstarch), chilli and ginger in a small bowl. Add to the saucepan, cover and simmer for 40 minutes, or until the

beans are tender and the sauce thickens. Stir occasionally.

3 Cut the aubergines (eggplants) into chunks and place in a colander. Sprinkle over the salt and leave to drain for 30 minutes. Rinse well to remove the salt and dry on paper towels.

4 Heat the oil in a preheated wok or large frying pan (skillet). Add the aubergine (eggplant) and garlic. Stir-fry for 3–4 minutes until the aubergine (eggplant) has started to brown.

5 Add the sauce to the aubergine (eggplant) chunks with the spring onions (scallions). Heat thoroughly and garnish with radish shreds.

TIME-SAVER

To save time, you can use a bottled black bean sauce instead of making your own. You will need about 6 tablespoonfuls.

STIR-FRIED MUSHROOMS, CUCUMBER & SMOKED TOFU (BEAN CURD)

Chunks of cucumber and smoked tofu (bean curd) stir-fried with straw mushrooms, mangetout (snow peas) and corn in a yellow bean sauce.

STEP 1

SERVES 4

1 large cucumber
1 tsp salt
225 g/7½ oz smoked tofu (bean curd)
2 tbsp vegetable oil
60 g/2 oz mangetout (snow peas)
125 g/4 oz/8 baby corn
1 celery stick, sliced diagonally
425 g/14 oz can straw mushrooms, rinsed
  and drained
2 spring onions (scallions), cut into strips
1 cm/½ inch piece ginger root, chopped
1 tbsp yellow bean sauce
1 tbsp light soy sauce
1 tbsp dry sherry

1 Halve the cucumber lengthways. Remove the seeds, using a teaspoon. Cut into cubes, place in a colander and sprinkle over the salt. Leave to drain for 10 minutes. Rinse thoroughly in cold water to remove the salt and drain thoroughly.

2 Cut the tofu (bean curd) into cubes. Heat the oil in a preheated wok or large frying pan (skillet). Add the tofu (bean curd), mangetout (snow peas), baby corn and celery. Stir until the tofu (bean curd) is lightly browned.

3 Add the straw mushrooms, spring onions (scallions) and ginger, and stir-fry for a further minute.

4 Stir in the cucumber, yellow bean sauce, soy sauce, sherry and 2 tablespoons water.

5 Continue to stir-fry for 1 minute more, then transfer to a serving plate and serve at once.

STRAW MUSHROOMS

Straw mushrooms are available in cans from Oriental suppliers and some supermarkets. If unavailable, substitute 250 g/8 oz baby button mushrooms.

STEP 2

STEP 3

STEP 4

STEP 2

STEP 3

STEP 4

STEP 6

VEGETABLE CASSEROLE WITH BLACK BEANS

This colourful Chinese-style casserole is made with tofu (bean curd), vegetables and black bean sauce.

SERVES 4

6 Chinese dried mushrooms (if unavailable,
    use thinly sliced open-cup mushrooms)
275 g/9 oz tofu (bean curd)
3 tbsp vegetable oil
1 carrot, cut into thin strips
125 g/4 oz mangetout (snow peas)
125 g/4 oz/8 baby corn, halved lengthways
225 g/7½ oz can sliced bamboo shoots,
    rinsed and drained
1 red (bell) pepper, cored, deseeded and cut
    into chunks
125 g/4 oz/1½ cups Chinese leaves,
    shredded
1 tbsp soy sauce
1 tbsp black bean sauce
1 tsp sugar
1 tsp cornflour (cornstarch)
vegetable oil for deep-frying
250 g/8 oz Chinese rice noodles
salt

1 Place the dried mushrooms in a small bowl and cover with warm water. Leave to soak for 20–25 minutes. Drain and squeeze out the excess water, reserving the liquid. Remove the tough centres and slice the mushrooms thinly.

2 Cut the tofu (bean curd) into cubes. Boil in a saucepan of lightly salted water for 2–3 minutes to firm up. Drain thoroughly.

3 Heat half the oil in a large flameproof casserole or saucepan. Add the tofu (bean curd) and fry until lightly browned all over. Remove with a perforated spoon and drain well on paper towels.

4 Add the remaining oil and stir-fry the mushrooms, carrot, mangetout (snow peas), baby corn, bamboo shoots and (bell) pepper for 2–3 minutes. Add the Chinese leaves and tofu (bean curd), and stir-fry for a further 2 minutes.

5 Stir in the soy sauce, black bean sauce and sugar, and season with salt. Add 6 tablespoons of the reserved mushroom liquid (or water if you are using ordinary mushrooms), mixed with cornflour (cornstarch). Bring to the boil, reduce the heat, cover and braise for 2–3 minutes until the sauce has thickened slightly.

6 Heat the oil for deep-frying in a large saucepan. Add the noodles in batches and deep-fry until puffed up and lightly golden. Drain on paper towels and serve with the casserole.

STEP 2

STEP 5

STEP 5

STEP 6

MONEY BAGS

These traditional steamed dumplings are made with a mushroom and sweetcorn (corn) filling. Eat them as they are, or try dipping them in a mixture of soy sauce, sherry and slivers of ginger root.

SERVES 4

3 Chinese dried mushrooms (if unavailable, use thinly sliced open-cup mushrooms)
250 g/8 oz/2 cups plain (all-purpose) flour
1 egg, beaten
75 ml/3 fl oz/6 tbsp water
1 tsp baking powder
¾ tsp salt
2 tbsp vegetable oil
2 spring onions (scallions), chopped
90 g/3 oz/½ cup sweetcorn (corn) kernels
½ red chilli, deseeded and chopped
1 tbsp brown bean sauce

1 Place the dried mushrooms in a small bowl, cover with warm water and leave to soak for 20–25 minutes.

2 To make the wrappers, sift the flour into a bowl. Add the egg and mix in lightly. Stir in the water, baking powder and salt. Mix to make a soft dough. Knead lightly until smooth on a floured board. Cover with a damp cloth and set aside for 5–6 minutes. This allows the baking powder time to activate, so that the dumplings swell when steaming.

3 Drain the mushrooms, squeezing them dry. Remove the tough centres and chop the mushrooms.

4 Heat the oil in a preheated wok or large frying pan (skillet). Add the mushrooms, spring onions (scallions), sweetcorn (corn) and chilli. Stir-fry for 2 minutes. Stir in the brown bean sauce and remove from the heat.

5 Roll the dough into a large sausage and cut into 24 even-sized pieces. Roll each piece out into a thin round and place a teaspoonful of the filling in the centre. Gather up the edges to a point, pinch together and twist to seal.

6 Stand the dumplings in an oiled steaming basket. Place over a saucepan of simmering water, cover and steam for 12–14 minutes before serving.

COOKING WITH CABBAGE LEAVES

For extra flavour and to help to prevent the dumplings falling through the steamer, place them on cabbage leaves inside the steamer.

CARROTS & PARSNIPS WITH COCONUT

Sliced carrots and chunks of parsnip are cooked in a creamy coconut sauce with ground almonds and served on a bed of spinach.

STEP 1

SERVES 2

90 g/3 oz/¹/₃ cup creamed coconut
300 ml/¹/₂ pint/1¹/₄ cups hot water
15 g/¹/₂ oz/2 tbsp flaked (slivered) almonds
4 tbsp vegetable oil
5 cardamom pods
4 thin slices ginger root
350 g/12 oz/2¹/₂ cups carrots, sliced
350 g/12 oz/2¹/₂ cups parsnips, cored and
    cut into small chunks
¹/₄ tsp Chinese five-spice powder
15 g/¹/₂ oz/2 tbsp ground almonds
200 g/7 oz/4 cups young spinach leaves
¹/₂ red onion, thinly sliced
1 garlic clove, sliced
salt

1 Crumble the creamed coconut into a bowl or jug, add the hot water and stir until dissolved.

2 Heat a saucepan and dry-fry the flaked (slivered) almonds until golden. Remove and set aside.

3 Heat half the oil in the saucepan. Add the cardamom pods and ginger root. Fry for 30 seconds to flavour the oil. Add the carrots and parsnips. Stir-fry for 2–3 minutes.

STEP 3

4 Stir in the five-spice powder and ground almonds, and pour in the coconut liquid. Bring to the boil and season with salt to taste. Cover and simmer for 12–15 minutes until the vegetables are tender. Stir occasionally, adding extra water if necessary.

5 Wash the spinach and drain thoroughly. Remove any stalks (stems). Heat the remaining oil in a preheated wok or large frying pan (skillet). Add the onion and garlic and stir-fry for 2 minutes. Add the spinach and stir-fry until it has just wilted. Drain off any excess liquid that has formed. Season with salt.

6 Remove the cardamom pods and ginger root from the carrots and parsnips, and adjust the seasoning. Serve on a bed of the spinach sprinkled with the almonds.

STEP 4

CARDAMOM

Lightly crush the cardamom pods before using, as this helps to release their flavour.

STEP 5

STEP 1

STEP 2

STEP 4

STEP 5

LENTIL BALLS WITH SWEET & SOUR SAUCE

Crisp golden lentil balls are served in a sweet and sour sauce with (bell) peppers and pineapple chunks.

SERVES 4

250 g/8 oz/1 cup red lentils
450 ml/³/₄ pint/scant 2 cups water
¹/₂ green chilli, deseeded and chopped
4 spring onions (scallions), finely chopped
1 garlic clove, crushed
1 tsp salt
4 tbsp pineapple juice from can
1 egg, beaten
vegetable oil for deep-frying

SAUCE:
3 tbsp white wine vinegar
2 tbsp sugar
2 tbsp tomato purée (paste)
1 tsp sesame oil
1 tsp cornflour (cornstarch)
¹/₂ tsp salt
6 tbsp water
2 canned pineapple rings
2 tbsp vegetable oil
¹/₂ red (bell) pepper, cut into chunks
¹/₂ green (bell) pepper, cut into chunks

1 Wash the lentils, then place in a saucepan with the water and bring to the boil. Skim and boil rapidly for 10 minutes, uncovered. Reduce the heat and simmer for 5 minutes until you have a fairly dry mixture. Considerably less water is used to cook these lentils than is normally required, so take care they do not burn as they cook. Stir occasionally.

2 Remove from the heat and stir in the chilli, spring onions (scallions), garlic, salt and pineapple juice. Leave to cool for 10 minutes.

3 To make the sauce, mix together the vinegar, sugar, tomato purée (paste), sesame oil, cornflour (cornstarch), salt and water, and set aside. Cut the pineapple into chunks.

4 Add the beaten egg to the lentil mixture. Heat the oil in a large saucepan or wok and deep-fry tablespoonfuls of the mixture in batches until crisp and golden. Remove with a perforated spoon and drain well on several layers of paper towels.

5 Heat the 2 tablespoons oil in a wok or frying pan (skillet). Stir-fry the (bell) peppers for 2 minutes. Add the sauce mixture with the pineapple chunks. Bring to the boil, then reduce the heat and simmer for 1 minute, stirring constantly, until the sauce has thickened. Add the lentil balls and heat thoroughly, taking care not to break them up. Serve with rice or noodles.

CHAPTER NINE

Vegetables & Salads

Due to the vast size of China, in which there are many different climates, the country produces a huge variety of vegetables. These play a significant role in the Chinese diet, and are considered important in their own right rather than as mere accompaniments.

Many Westerners overcook their vegetables, boiling them in too much water and causing them to lose all their flavours and colours as well as their valuable vitamins and minerals. Stir-frying was until recently a method of cooking unique to the Chinese. The raw ingredients are cooked quickly with a minimum of oil or water over a high heat. This ensures that flavours, colours and nutrients are preserved leaving the vegetables crisp and colourful.

A mixture of raw and cooked vegetables is often used in Chinese salads, and these are picked fresh as they are needed. Choose firm crisp vegetables and cook them while they are at their best, as this will make all the difference to your final dish.

Opposite: *A tempting array of fresh fruits and vegetables in the western district of Hong Kong.*

STEP 1

STEP 2

STEP 4

STEP 5

AUBERGINES (EGGPLANTS) IN CHILLI SAUCE

Strips of aubergine (eggplant) are deep-fried, then served in a fragrant chilli sauce with carrot matchsticks and spring onions (scallions).

SERVES 4

1 large aubergine (eggplant)
vegetable oil for deep-frying
2 carrots
4 spring onions (scallions)
2 large garlic cloves
1 tbsp vegetable oil
2 tsp chilli sauce
1 tbsp soy sauce
1 tbsp dry sherry

1 Slice the aubergine (eggplant) and then cut into strips about the size of potato chips (French fries).

2 Heat enough oil in a large heavy-based saucepan to deep-fry the aubergine (eggplant) in batches until just browned. Remove the strips with a perforated spoon and drain them on paper towels.

3 Cut the carrots into thin matchsticks. Trim and slice the spring onions (scallions) diagonally. Slice the garlic cloves.

4 Heat 1 tablespoon oil in a wok or large frying pan (skillet). Add the carrot matchsticks and stir-fry for 1 minute, then add the chopped spring onions (scallions) and garlic and stir-fry for a further minute.

5 Stir in the chilli sauce, soy sauce and sherry, then stir in the drained aubergine (eggplant) strips. Mix well to ensure that the vegetables are heated through thoroughly before serving.

MILDER FLAVOUR

For a milder dish, substitute hoi-sin sauce for the chilli sauce. This can be bought ready-made from all supermarkets.

STEP 1

STEP 2

STEP 3

STEP 4

GINGERED BROCCOLI WITH ORANGE

Thinly sliced broccoli florets are lightly stir-fried and served in a ginger and orange sauce.

SERVES 4

750 g/1½ lb broccoli
2 thin slices ginger root
2 garlic cloves
1 orange
2 tsp cornflour (cornstarch)
1 tbsp light soy sauce
½ tsp sugar
2 tbsp vegetable oil

1 Divide the broccoli into small florets. Peel the stalks (stems), using a vegetable peeler, and then cut them into thin slices. Cut the ginger root into matchsticks and slice the garlic.

2 Peel 2 long strips of rind from the orange and cut into thin strips. Place the strips in a bowl, cover with cold water and set aside. Squeeze the juice from the orange and mix with the cornflour (cornstarch), soy sauce, sugar and 4 tablespoons water.

3 Heat the oil in a wok or large frying pan (skillet). Add the broccoli stalk (stem) slices and stir-fry for 2 minutes. Add the ginger root slices, garlic and broccoli florets, and stir-fry for a further 3 minutes.

4 Stir in the orange sauce mixture and cook, stirring constantly, until the sauce has thickened and coated the broccoli.

5 Drain the reserved orange rind and stir in before serving.

> ### VARIATION
>
> This dish could be made with cauliflower, if you prefer, or a mixture of cauliflower and broccoli.

LEMON CHINESE LEAVES

These stir-fried Chinese leaves are served with a tangy sauce made of grated lemon rind, lemon juice and ginger.

STEP 1

SERVES 4

500 g/1 lb Chinese leaves
3 tbsp vegetable oil
1 cm/¹/₂ inch piece ginger root, grated
1 tsp salt
1 tsp sugar
120 ml/4 fl oz/¹/₂ cup water or vegetable
    stock
1 tsp grated lemon rind
1 tbsp cornflour (cornstarch)
1 tbsp lemon juice

1 Separate the Chinese leaves, wash and drain thoroughly. Pat dry with paper towels. Cut into 5 cm/2 inch wide slices.

2 Heat the oil in a preheated wok or large frying pan (skillet). Add the grated ginger root, followed by the Chinese leaves. Stir-fry for 2–3 minutes or until the leaves begin to wilt. Add the salt and sugar, and mix well until the leaves soften. Remove the leaves with a perforated spoon and set aside.

3 Add the water or vegetable stock to the pan with the grated lemon rind and bring to the boil. Meanwhile, mix the cornflour (cornstarch) to a smooth paste with the lemon juice, then add to the

water or stock in the pan. Simmer, stirring constantly, for about 1 minute to make a smooth sauce.

4 Return the cooked leaves to the pan and mix thoroughly. Arrange on a serving plate and serve immediately.

STEP 2

STEP 3

CHINESE LEAVES

If Chinese leaves are unavailable, substitute slices of savoy cabbage. Cook for 1 extra minute to soften the leaves.

STEP 4

STEP 1

STEP 2

STEP 3

STEP 4

GOLDEN NEEDLES WITH BAMBOO SHOOTS

Golden needles are the dried flower buds of the tiger lily. They are usually sold in the dried form and can be obtained from specialist Chinese stores. They give a unique musky flavour to this dish.

SERVES 4

30 g/1 oz/¹/₄ cup dried lily flowers
2 × 225 g/7¹/₂ oz cans bamboo shoots,
    rinsed and drained
60 g/2 oz/¹/₂ cup cornflour (cornstarch)
vegetable oil for deep-frying
1 tbsp vegetable oil
450ml/³/₄ pint/scant 2 cups vegetable stock
1 tbsp dark soy sauce
1 tbsp dry sherry
1 tsp sugar
1 large garlic clove, sliced
¹/₂ each red, green and yellow (bell) peppers

1 Soak the lily flowers in hot water for 30 minutes.

2 Coat the bamboo shoots in cornflour (cornstarch). Heat enough oil in a large heavy-based saucepan to deep-fry the bamboo shoots in batches until just beginning to colour. Remove with a perforated spoon and drain on paper towels.

3 Drain the lily flowers and trim off the hard ends. Heat 1 tablespoon oil in a wok or large frying pan (skillet). Add the lily flowers, bamboo shoots, stock, soy sauce, sherry, sugar and garlic.

4 Slice the (bell) peppers thinly and add to the pan. Bring to the boil, stirring constantly, then reduce the heat and simmer for 5 minutes. Add extra water or stock if necessary.

COATING THE BAMBOO SHOOTS

To coat the bamboo shoots easily with cornflour (cornstarch), place the cornflour (cornstarch) in a plastic bag, add the bamboo shoots in batches and shake well.

STEP 1

STEP 3

STEP 4

STEP 5

SPINACH WITH STRAW MUSHROOMS

Straw mushrooms are available in cans from Oriental stores. Here they are served with spinach, raisins and pine kernels (nuts). You can use button mushrooms instead, if straw mushrooms are unavailable.

SERVES 4

30 g/1 oz/¼ cup pine kernels (nuts)
500 g/1 lb fresh spinach leaves
3 tbsp vegetable oil
1 red onion, sliced
2 garlic cloves, sliced
425 g/14 oz can straw mushrooms, rinsed
   and drained
30 g/1 oz/3 tbsp raisins
2 tbsp soy sauce
salt

1 Heat a wok or large frying pan (skillet) and dry-fry the pine kernels (nuts) until lightly browned. Remove and set aside.

2 Wash the spinach thoroughly, picking the leaves over and removing long stalks (stems). Drain and pat dry with paper towels.

3 Heat the oil in the preheated wok or frying pan (skillet). Add the onion and garlic, and stir-fry for 1 minute.

4 Add the spinach and mushrooms, and continue to stir-fry until the leaves have wilted. Drain off all the excess liquid.

5 Stir in the raisins, reserved pine kernels (nuts) and soy sauce. Stir-fry until thoroughly heated and well-mixed. Season to taste with salt before serving.

ADDING FLAVOUR

Soak the raisins in 2 tablespoons dry sherry before using. This helps to plump them up as well as adding extra flavour to the stir-fry.

GADO GADO SALAD

This salad is a mixture of cooked and raw vegetables in a spicy peanut dressing. The vegetables can either be arranged in individual piles on the serving platter or mixed together.

STEP 2

SERVES 4

250 g/8 oz new potatoes, scrubbed
125 g/4 oz green beans
125 g/4 oz cauliflower, broken into small
   florets
125 g/4 oz/1½ cups white cabbage,
   shredded
1 carrot, cut into thin sticks
¼ cucumber, cut into chunks
125 g/4 oz/2 cups bean-sprouts
2 hard-boiled (hard-cooked) eggs

SAUCE:
6 tbsp crunchy peanut butter
300 ml/½ pint/1¼ cups cold water
1 garlic clove, crushed
1 fresh red chilli, deseeded and finely
   chopped
2 tbsp soy sauce
1 tbsp dry sherry
2 tsp sugar
1 tbsp lemon juice

1 Halve the potatoes and place in a saucepan of lightly salted water. Bring to the boil and then simmer for 12–15 minutes or until cooked through. Drain and plunge into cold water to cool.

2 Bring another pan of lightly salted water to the boil. Add the green beans, cauliflower and cabbage, and cook for 3 minutes. Drain and plunge the vegetables into cold water to cool and prevent any further cooking.

3 Drain the potatoes and other cooked vegetables. Arrange in piles on a large serving platter with the carrot, cucumber and bean-sprouts.

4 Remove the shells from the hard-boiled (hard-cooked) eggs, cut into quarters and arrange on the salad. Cover and set aside.

5 To make the sauce, place the peanut butter in a bowl and blend in the water gradually, followed by the remaining ingredients.

6 Uncover the salad, place the sauce in a separate serving bowl and drizzle some over each serving.

STEP 3

STEP 4

COCONUT MILK

For extra flavour in the peanut sauce, use coconut milk instead of water. This can be purchased from specialist Oriental stores and some supermarkets.

STEP 5

STEP 1

STEP 2

STEP 3

STEP 4

ORIENTAL SALAD

This colourful crisp salad has a fresh orange dressing and is topped with crunchy vermicelli.

SERVES 4–6

30 g/1 oz/¼ cup dried vermicelli
½ head Chinese leaves
125 g/4 oz/2 cups bean-sprouts
6 radishes
125 g/4 oz mangetout (snow peas)
1 large carrot
125 g/4 oz sprouting beans

DRESSING:
juice of 1 orange
1 tbsp sesame seeds, toasted
1 tsp honey
1 tsp sesame oil
1 tbsp hazelnut oil

1 Break the vermicelli into small strands. Heat a wok or frying pan (skillet) and dry-fry the vermicelli until lightly golden. Remove from the pan and set aside.

2 Shred the Chinese leaves and wash with the bean-sprouts. Drain thoroughly and place in a large bowl. Slice the radishes. Trim the mangetout (snow peas) and cut each into 3 pieces. Cut the carrot into thin matchsticks. Add the sprouting beans and prepared vegetables to the bowl.

3 Place all the dressing ingredients in a screw-top jar and shake until well-blended. Pour over the salad and toss together well.

4 Transfer the salad to a serving bowl and sprinkle over the reserved vermicelli before serving.

SPROUTING BEANS

If you are unable to buy sprouting beans, you can make your own. Use a mixture of mung and aduki beans and chick-peas (garbanzo beans). Soak the beans overnight in cold water, drain and rinse. Place in a large glass jam jar and cover the mouth of the jar with a piece of muslin (cheesecloth) tied on to secure it. Lay the jar on its side and place in indirect light. For the next 2–3 days rinse the beans once each day in cold water until they are ready to eat.

CHAPTER TEN

Rice & Noodles

Rice and noodles form the central part of most Oriental meals, particularly in the southern part of China. In the north the staple foods tend to contain more wheat-based products, such as dumplings. Rice and noodles supply the carbohydrate necessary for a nutritious meal, and though bland in themselves they provide a complementary texture to the other ingredients and absorb the stronger flavours of other dishes, making them an essential and very satisfying part of the Chinese meal.

The most common types of rice used in Chinese cuisine include white or brown long-grain rice and glutinous rice. The shorter grain of the glutinous rice has a slight stickiness when cooked, which makes it ideal for eating with chopsticks.

Rice can be boiled and then steamed, or it can be fried with other ingredients added, such as scrambled eggs, spring onions (scallions) or peas, then flavoured with soy sauce. It is also used to make wines, vinegars, noodles and flour, which makes it a very important ingredient.

A wide variety of Chinese noodles are available, made from wheat, buckwheat or rice flours. Like rice, they are very versatile; they can be boiled or fried, and served plain with a sauce, or in a soup.

Opposite: *A 1000-year old banyan tree overhangs a rice field in the Guangxi province.*

STEP 1

STEP 3

STEP 4

STEP 5

HOMEMADE NOODLES WITH STIR-FRIED VEGETABLES

These noodles are simple to make; you do not need a pasta-making machine as they are rolled out by hand.

SERVES 2–4

NOODLES:
125 g/4 oz/1 cup plain (all-purpose) flour
2 tbsp cornflour (cornstarch)
¹/₂ tsp salt
120 ml/4 fl oz/¹/₂ cup boiling water
5 tbsp vegetable oil

STIR-FRY:
1 courgette (zucchini)
1 celery stick
1 carrot
125 g/4 oz open-cup mushrooms
1 leek
125 g/4 oz broccoli
125 g/4 oz/2 cups bean-sprouts
1 tbsp soy sauce
2 tsp rice wine vinegar (if unavailable, use white wine vinegar)
¹/₂ tsp sugar

1 To prepare the noodles, sift the flour, cornflour (cornstarch) and salt into a bowl. Make a well in the centre and pour in the boiling water and 1 teaspoon of the oil. Mix quickly, using a wooden spoon, to make a soft dough. Cover and leave for 5–6 minutes.

2 Prepare the vegetables for the stir-fry. Cut the courgette (zucchini),

celery and carrot into thin sticks. Slice the mushrooms and leek. Divide the broccoli into small florets and peel and thinly slice the stalks (stems).

3 Make the noodles by breaking off small pieces of dough and rolling into balls. Then roll each ball across a very lightly oiled work surface (counter) with the palm of your hand to form thin noodles. Do not worry if some of the noodles break into shorter lengths. Set the noodles aside.

4 Heat 3 tablespoons of oil in a wok or large frying pan (skillet). Add the noodles in batches and fry over a high heat for 1 minute. Reduce the heat and cook for a further 2 minutes. Remove and drain on paper towels. Set aside.

5 Heat the remaining oil in the pan. Add the courgette (zucchini), celery and carrot, and stir-fry for 1 minute. Add the mushrooms, broccoli and leek, and stir-fry for a further minute. Stir in the remaining ingredients and mix well until thoroughly heated.

6 Add the noodles and toss to mix together over a high heat. Serve immediately.

STEP 2

STEP 3

STEP 4

STEP 5

VEGETABLE CHOW MEIN

Chinese egg noodles are fried with a colourful variety of vegetables to make this well-known dish.

SERVES 4

500 g/ 1 lb egg noodles
4 tbsp vegetable oil
1 onion, thinly sliced
2 carrots, cut into thin sticks
125 g/4 oz/1⅓ cups button mushrooms, quartered
125 g/4 oz mangetout (snow peas)
½ cucumber, cut into sticks
125 g/4 oz/ 2 cups spinach, shredded
125 g/4 oz/ 2 cups bean-sprouts
2 tbsp dark soy sauce
1 tbsp sherry
1 tsp salt
1 tsp sugar
1 tsp cornflour (cornstarch)
1 tsp sesame oil

1 Cook the noodles according to the packet instructions. Drain and rinse under running cold water until cool. Set aside.

2 Heat 3 tablespoons of the vegetable oil in a wok or large frying pan (skillet). Add the onion and carrots, and stir-fry for 1 minute. Add the mushroom quarters, mangetout (snow peas) and cucumber, and stir-fry for a further 1 minute.

3 Stir in the remaining vegetable oil and add the drained noodles with the spinach and bean-sprouts.

4 Blend together the remaining ingredients and pour over the noodles and vegetables.

5 Stir-fry until thoroughly heated and serve.

FOR A HOTTER FLAVOUR

For a spicy hot chow mein, add 1 tablespoon chilli sauce or substitute chilli oil for the sesame oil.

VEGETARIAN FRIED RICE

In this simple recipe, cooked rice is fried with vegetables and cashew nuts. It can either be eaten on its own or served as an accompaniment.

STEP 2

STEP 3

STEP 4

STEP 4

SERVES 2–4

175 g/6 oz/generous ³/₄ cup long-grain rice
60 g/2 oz/¹/₂ cup cashew nuts
1 carrot
¹/₂ cucumber
1 yellow (bell) pepper
2 spring onions (scallions)
2 tbsp vegetable oil
1 garlic clove, crushed
125 g/4 oz/³/₄ cup frozen peas, defrosted
1 tbsp soy sauce
1 tsp salt
coriander (cilantro) leaves, to garnish

1 Bring a large pan of water to the boil. Add the rice and simmer for 15 minutes. Tip the rice into a sieve (strainer) and rinse; drain thoroughly.

2 Heat a wok or large frying pan (skillet). Add the cashew nuts and dry-fry until lightly browned. Remove and set aside.

3 Cut the carrot in half along the length, then slice thinly into semi-circles. Halve the cucumber and remove the seeds, using a teaspoon; dice the cucumber. Slice the (bell) pepper and chop the spring onions (scallions).

4 Heat the oil in the wok or large frying pan (skillet). Add the prepared vegetables and the garlic. Stir-fry for 3 minutes. Add the rice, peas, soy sauce and salt. Continue to stir-fry until well mixed and thoroughly heated.

5 Stir in the reserved cashew nuts and serve garnished with coriander (cilantro) leaves.

LAST-MINUTE MEAL

You can replace any of the vegetables in this recipe with others suitable for a stir-fry, and using leftover rice makes this a perfect last-minute dish.

STEP 1

STEP 4

STEP 5

STEP 6

FRAGRANT STEAMED RICE IN LOTUS LEAVES

The fragrance of the leaves penetrates the rice, giving it a unique taste. Lotus leaves can be bought from specialist Chinese stores. Large cabbage or spinach leaves can be used as a substitute.

SERVES 4

2 lotus leaves
4 Chinese dried mushrooms (if unavailable,
    use thinly sliced open-cup mushrooms)
175 g/6 oz/generous ¾ cup long-grain rice
1 cinnamon stick
6 cardamom pods
4 cloves
1 tsp salt
2 eggs
1 tbsp vegetable oil
2 spring onions (scallions), chopped
1 tbsp soy sauce
2 tbsp sherry
1 tsp sugar
1 tsp sesame oil

1 Unfold the lotus leaves carefully and cut along the fold to divide each leaf in half. Lay on a large baking tray and pour over enough hot water to cover. Leave to soak for about 30 minutes or until the leaves have softened.

2 Place the dried mushrooms in a small bowl and cover with warm water. Leave to soak for 20–25 minutes.

3 Cook the rice in plenty of boiling water in a saucepan with the cinnamon stick, cardamom pods, cloves and salt for about 10 minutes – the rice should be partially cooked. Drain thoroughly and remove the cinnamon.

4 Beat the eggs lightly. Heat the oil in a preheated wok or frying pan (skillet) and cook the eggs quickly, stirring constantly until they are set; then remove and set aside.

5 Drain the mushrooms, squeezing out the excess water. Remove the tough centres and chop the mushrooms. Place the rice in a bowl. Stir in the mushrooms, cooked egg, spring onions (scallions), soy sauce, sherry, sugar and sesame oil. Season with salt to taste.

6 Drain the lotus leaves and divide the rice mixture into 4 portions. Place a portion in the centre of each lotus leaf and fold up to form a parcel. Place in a steamer, cover and steam over simmering water for 20 minutes. To serve, cut the tops of the lotus leaves open to expose the fragrant rice inside.

STEP 1

STEP 2

STEP 3

STEP 5

SPICY COCONUT RICE WITH GREEN LENTILS

Rice and green lentils are cooked with creamed coconut, lemon grass and curry leaves. This recipe will serve two people as a main course or four as an accompaniment.

SERVES 2–4

90 g/ 3 oz/$^1/_3$ cup green lentils
250 g/8 oz/generous 1 cup long-grain rice
2 tbsp vegetable oil
1 onion, sliced
2 garlic cloves, crushed
3 curry leaves
1 stalk lemon grass, chopped (if unavailable,
    use grated rind of $^1/_2$ lemon)
1 green chilli, deseeded and chopped
$^1/_2$ tsp cumin seeds
1$^1/_2$ tsp salt
90 g/3 oz/$^1/_3$ cup creamed coconut
600 ml/1 pint/2$^1/_2$ cups hot water
2 tbsp chopped fresh coriander (cilantro)

TO GARNISH:
shredded radishes
shredded cucumber

1 Wash the lentils and place in a saucepan. Cover with cold water, bring to the boil and boil rapidly for 10 minutes. Wash the rice thoroughly and drain well.

2 Heat the oil in a large saucepan, which has a tight-fitting lid, and fry the onion for 3–4 minutes. Add the garlic, curry leaves, lemon grass, chilli, cumin seeds and salt, and stir well.

3 Drain the lentils and rinse. Add to the onion and spices with the rice and mix well. Add the creamed coconut to the hot water and stir until dissolved. Stir into the rice mixture and bring to the boil. Turn down the heat to low, put the lid on tightly and leave to cook undisturbed for 15 minutes.

4 Without removing the lid, remove the pan from the heat and leave to rest for 10 minutes to allow the rice and lentils to finish cooking in their own steam.

5 Stir in the coriander (cilantro) and remove the curry leaves. Serve garnished with shredded radishes and cucumber.

CREAMED COCONUT

If creamed coconut is unavailable, use 60 g/2 oz/$^2/_3$ cup desiccated (shredded) coconut. Infuse it in the hot water for 20 minutes, drain well and squeeze out any excess water. Discard the coconut and use the liquid.

STEP 2

STEP 3

STEP 5

STEP 6

EGG FU-YUNG WITH RICE

In this dish, cooked rice is mixed with scrambled eggs, Chinese mushrooms, bamboo shoots and water chestnuts, and it is a great way of using up leftover cooked rice. It can be served as a meal by itself or as an accompaniment.

SERVES 2–4

175 g/6 oz/generous ³/₄ cup long-grain rice
2 Chinese dried mushrooms (if unavailable, use thinly sliced open-cup mushrooms)
3 eggs, beaten
3 tbsp vegetable oil
4 spring onions (scallions), sliced
¹/₂ green (bell) pepper, cored, deseeded and chopped
60 g/2 oz/¹/₃ cup canned bamboo shoots, rinsed and drained
60 g/2 oz/¹/₃ cup canned water chestnuts, rinsed, drained and sliced
125 g/4 oz/2 cups bean-sprouts
2 tbsp light soy sauce
2 tbsp dry sherry
2 tsp sesame oil
salt and pepper

1 Cook the rice in lightly salted boiling water according to the packet instructions.

2 Place the dried mushrooms in a small bowl, cover with warm water and leave to soak for 20–25 minutes.

3 Mix the beaten eggs with a little salt. Heat 1 tablespoon of the oil in a wok or large frying pan (skillet). Add the eggs and stir until just set. Remove and set aside.

4 Drain the mushrooms and squeeze out the excess water. Remove the tough centres and chop the mushrooms.

5 Heat the remaining oil in a clean wok or frying pan (skillet). Add the mushrooms, spring onions (scallions) and green (bell) pepper, and stir-fry for 2 minutes. Add the bamboo shoots, water chestnuts and bean-sprouts. Stir-fry for 1 minute.

6 Drain the rice thoroughly and add to the pan with the remaining ingredients. Mix well, heating the rice thoroughly. Season to taste with salt and pepper. Stir in the reserved eggs and serve at once.

WASHING BEAN-SPROUTS

To wash bean-sprouts, place them in a bowl of cold water and swirl with your hand. Remove any long tail ends.

APPETIZERS

•

SOUPS

•

SEAFOOD DISHES

•

MEAT & POULTRY DISHES

•

**VEGETABLES, RICE &
NOODLES**

3

SZECHUAN COOKING

CHAPTER ELEVEN

Appetizers

Appetizers are often served as the first course or for nibbles with drinks in Szechuan – just like hors d'oeuvres in the West. The advantage of these dishes is that they can generally be prepared and even cooked well in advance – hours before serving if need be. Also, almost all the dishes selected here are ideal for a buffet-style meal or as party food.

Instead of serving a selection of appetizers individually, you can serve a small portion of several or all together as an assortment. Select a minimum of three different items such as Deep-fried Prawns (Shrimp), Bang-bang Chicken, Deep-fried Spare Ribs and so on.

Other dishes that can be served as a part of the appetizer selection are Szechuan Prawns (Shrimp), Sweet & Sour Prawns (Shrimp), Aromatic & Crispy Duck, and Braised Chinese Leaves. Remember not to have more than one of the same type of food, and the ingredients should be chosen for their harmony and balance in colour, aroma, flavour and texture.

Opposite: *The Great Wall snakes across many miles of this vast country.*

STEP 1

STEP 2

STEP 3

STEP 4

DEEP-FRIED PRAWNS (SHRIMP)

For best results, use raw tiger prawns (or jumbo shrimp) in their shells. They are 7–10 cm/3–4 inches long, and you should get 18–20 prawns (shrimp) per 500 g/1 lb.

SERVES 4

250–300 g/8–10 oz raw prawns (shrimp) in their shells, defrosted if frozen
1 tbsp light soy sauce
1 tsp Chinese rice wine or dry sherry
2 tsp cornflour (cornstarch)
vegetable oil for deep-frying
2–3 spring onions (scallions), to garnish

SPICY SALT AND PEPPER:
1 tbsp salt
1 tsp ground Szechuan peppercorns
1 tsp Chinese five-spice powder

1 Pull the soft legs off the prawns (shrimp), but keep the body shell on. Dry well on paper towels.

2 Place the prawns (shrimp) in a bowl with the soy sauce, wine and cornflour (cornstarch). Turn to coat and leave to marinate for about 25–30 minutes.

3 To make the Spicy Salt and Pepper, mix the salt, pepper and five-spice powder together. Place in a dry frying pan (skillet) and stir-fry for 3–4 minutes over a low heat, stirring constantly. Remove from the heat and allow to cool.

4 Heat the oil in a preheated wok until smoking, then deep-fry the prawns (shrimp) in batches until golden brown. Remove with a slotted spoon and drain on paper towels.

5 Place the spring onions (scallions) in a bowl, pour on 1 tablespoon of the hot oil and leave for 30 seconds. Serve the prawns (shrimp) garnished with the spring onions (scallions), and with Spicy Salt and Pepper as a dip.

ROASTING SPICES

The roasted spice mixture made with Szechuan peppercorns is used throughout China as a dip for deep-fried food. The peppercorns are sometimes roasted first and then ground. Dry-frying is a way of releasing the flavours of the spices. You can make the dip in advance and store in a tightly sealed jar until ready to use.

STEP 1

STEP 2

STEP 3

STEP 4

PORK WITH CHILLI & GARLIC SAUCE

*Any leftovers from this dish can be used for a number of other dishes –
such as Hot & Sour Soup (see page 170), and Twice-cooked Pork
(see page 203).*

SERVES 4

*500 g/ 1 lb leg of pork, boned but not
skinned*

SAUCE:
1 tsp finely chopped garlic
*1 tsp finely chopped spring onions
(scallions)*
2 tbsp light soy sauce
1 tsp red chilli oil
1/2 tsp sesame oil

1 Place the pork, tied together in one piece, in a large pan, add enough cold water to cover and bring to a rolling boil over a medium heat.

2 Skim off the scum that rises to the surface, cover and simmer gently for 25–30 minutes.

3 Leave the meat in the liquid to cool, under cover, for at least 1–2 hours. Lift out the meat with 2 slotted spoons and leave to cool completely, skin-side up, for 2–3 hours.

4 To serve, cut off the skin, leaving a very thin layer of fat on top like a ham joint. Cut the meat in small thin slices across the grain, and arrange

neatly on a plate. Mix together the sauce ingredients, and pour the sauce evenly over the pork.

SZECHUAN CHILLI

One of the local Szechuan plants that contributes most to the typical character of the region's cooking is the small red fagara chilli, which is used both fresh and dried. The chilli has a delayed action on the palate; at first it seems to have little taste, but suddenly it burns the mouth with great ferocity, so it is used with much respect. It is claimed that instead of burning the taste-buds, the chilli actually makes them more sensitive to other flavours.

This is a very simple dish, but beautifully presented. Make sure you slice the meat as thinly and evenly as possible to make an elegantly arranged dish.

BANG-BANG CHICKEN

The cooked chicken meat is tenderized by being beaten with a rolling pin, hence the name for this very popular Szechuan dish.

SERVES 4

1 litre/1³/₄ pints/4 cups water
2 chicken quarters (breast half and leg)
1 cucumber, cut into matchstick shreds

SAUCE:
2 tbsp light soy sauce
1 tsp sugar
1 tbsp finely chopped spring onions
  (scallions)
1 tsp red chilli oil
¹/₄ tsp pepper
1 tsp white sesame seeds
2 tbsp peanut butter, creamed with a little
  sesame oil

1 Bring the water to a rolling boil in a wok or a large pan. Add the chicken pieces, reduce the heat, cover and simmer for 30–35 minutes.

2 Remove the chicken from the pan and immerse it in a bowl of cold water for at least 1 hour to cool it, ready for shredding.

3 Remove the chicken pieces and drain well. Dry the chicken pieces on absorbent kitchen paper (paper towels), then take the meat off the bone.

4 On a flat surface, pound the chicken with a rolling pin, then tear the meat into shreds with 2 forks. Mix with the shredded cucumber and arrange in a serving dish.

5 To serve, mix together all the sauce ingredients and pour over the chicken and cucumber.

THE CHOICEST CHICKEN

This dish is also known as Bon-bon Chicken – *bon* is a Chinese work for stick, so again the tenderizing technique inspires the recipe name.

Take the time to tear the chicken meat into similar-sized shreds, to make an elegant-looking dish. You can do this quite efficiently with 2 forks, although Chinese cooks would do it with their fingers.

STEP 1

STEP 1

STEP 2

STEP 3

PICKLED CUCUMBER

The pickling takes minutes rather than days – but the longer you leave it, the better the result. Some pickled vegetables are marinated for days – see the recipe for Mixed Pickled Vegetables, below.

SERVES 4

1 slender cucumber, about 30 cm/12 inches long
1 tsp salt
2 tsp caster (superfine) sugar
1 tsp rice vinegar
1 tsp red chilli oil
a few drops sesame oil

1 Halve the cucumber, unpeeled, lengthways. Scrape off the seeds and cut across into thick chunks.

2 Sprinkle with the salt and mix well. Leave to marinate for at least 20–30 minutes, longer if possible, then pour the juice away.

3 Mix the cucumber with the sugar, vinegar and chilli oil, and sprinkle with the sesame oil just before serving.

MIXED PICKLED VEGETABLES

350 g/12 oz Chinese leaves, cut into bite-sized pieces
50 g/2 oz French (green) beans, topped and tailed
125 g/4 oz carrots, diced
3 chillies, deseeded and finely chopped
2 tsp Szechuan peppercorns
2 tbsp coarse salt
2 tbsp rice wine

Place the vegetables in a glass bowl with the chillies, peppercorns, salt and wine. Stir well, cover and leave to marinate in the refrigerator for 4 days. Serve cold, as a salad.

PICKLED VEGETABLES

Pickled vegetables and fruits are very popular with the Chinese. They are often served as snacks and appetizers, and can also be served with cold meat dishes. Usually, the vegetables are allowed to stay in the marinade for 3–4 days. Once made, they will keep in the refrigerator for up to 2 weeks.

STEP 1

STEP 2

STEP 3

STEP 4

DEEP-FRIED SPARE RIBS

The spare ribs should be chopped into small bite-sized pieces before or after cooking.

SERVES 4

8–10 finger spare ribs
1 tsp Chinese five-spice powder or 1 tbsp
    mild curry powder
1 tbsp rice wine or dry sherry
1 egg
2 tbsp plain (all-purpose) flour
vegetable oil for deep-frying
1 tsp finely shredded spring onions
    (scallions)
1 tsp finely shredded fresh green or red hot
    chillies, deseeded
salt and pepper
Spicy Salt and Pepper (see page 158),
    to serve

1 Chop the ribs into 3–4 small pieces. Place the ribs in a bowl with salt, pepper, five-spice or curry powder and the wine. Turn to coat the ribs in the spices and leave them to marinate for 1–2 hours.

2 Mix the egg and flour together to make a batter.

3 Dip the ribs in the batter one by one to coat well.

4 Heat the oil in a preheated wok until smoking. Deep-fry the ribs for 4–5 minutes, then remove with a slotted spoon and drain on paper towels.

5 Reheat the oil over a high heat and deep-fry the ribs once more for another minute. Remove and drain again on paper towels.

6 Pour 1 tablespoon of the hot oil over the spring onions (scallions) and chillies and leave for 30–40 seconds. Serve the ribs with Spicy Salt and Pepper, garnished with the shredded spring onions (scallions) and chillies.

FINGER RIBS

To make finger ribs, cut the sheet of spare ribs into individual ribs down each side of the bones. These ribs are then chopped into bite-sized pieces for deep-frying.

CHAPTER TWELVE

Soups

Soup is not normally served as a separate course in China,
except at formal occasions and banquets, when it usually appears
towards the end of the meal.

Otherwise, in Chinese homes a simply made soup is served
with all the other dishes throughout the meal. The soup is
almost always a clear broth in which some thinly sliced vegetables
and/or meat have been poached quickly.

The soup should ideally be made with a good stock. If you use a
stock cube, remember to reduce the amount of seasoning
in the recipes, since most commercially made bouillon
cubes are fairly salty and spicy. It is always worth while making
your own Chinese stock, following the recipe on page 230,
if you have the time.

*Opposite: Fresh vegetables on
display in a market in
Szechuan. The Chinese shop
daily in the markets to ensure
that produce is absolutely fresh
and crisp.*

STEP 1

STEP 2

STEP 3

STEP 4

HOT & SOUR SOUP

This is the favourite soup in Chinese restaurants throughout the world.

SERVES 4

4-6 dried Chinese mushrooms (shiitake),
   soaked
125 g/4 oz cooked pork or chicken
1 cake tofu (bean curd)
60 g/2 oz canned sliced bamboo shoots,
   rinsed and drained
600 ml/1 pint/2½ cups Chinese Stock
   (see page 230) or water
1 tbsp Chinese rice wine or dry sherry
1 tbsp light soy sauce
2 tbsp rice vinegar
1 tbsp cornflour (cornstarch) paste
   (see page 231)
salt, to taste
½ tsp ground white pepper
2-3 spring onions (scallions), thinly sliced,
   to serve

1 Drain the mushrooms, squeeze dry and discard the hard stalks (stems). Thinly slice the mushrooms.

2 Thinly slice the meat, tofu (bean curd) and bamboo shoots into narrow shreds.

3 Bring the stock or water to a rolling boil in a wok or large saucepan and add all the ingredients. Bring back to the boil, then simmer for about 1 minute.

4 Add the wine, soy sauce and vinegar and bring back to the boil once more, stirring. Using a wooden spoon, stir in the cornflour (cornstarch) paste to thicken the soup. Serve hot, sprinkled with the thinly sliced spring onions (scallions).

DRIED MUSHROOMS

There are many varieties of dried mushrooms, which add a particular flavour to Chinese cooking. Shiitake mushrooms are one of the favourite kinds to use. Soak in hot water for 25–30 minutes before use and cut off the hard stalks (stems).

If you strain the soaking liquid through fine muslin (cheesecloth), you can use the liquid to give a mushroom flavour to other soups, as well as sauces and casseroles. It is important to strain the liquid carefully because it will contain small, gritty particles.

STEP 1

STEP 1

STEP 2

STEP 3

THREE-FLAVOUR SOUP

Ideally, use raw prawns (shrimp) in this soup. If that is not possible, add ready-cooked ones at the very last stage.

SERVES 4

125 g/4 oz skinned, boned chicken breast
125 g/4 oz raw peeled prawns (shrimp)
salt
½ egg white, lightly beaten
2 tsp cornflour (cornstarch) paste
   (see page 231)
125 g/4 oz honey-roast ham
750 ml/1¼ pints/3 cups Chinese Stock
   (see page 230) or water
finely chopped spring onions (scallions), to
   garnish

1 Thinly slice the chicken into small shreds. If the prawns (shrimp) are large, cut each in half lengthways, otherwise leave whole. Place the chicken and prawns (shrimps) in a bowl and mix with a pinch of salt, the egg white and cornflour (cornstarch) paste until well coated.

2 Cut the ham into small thin slices roughly the same size as the chicken pieces.

3 Bring the stock or water to a rolling boil, add the chicken, the raw prawns (shrimps) and the ham. Bring the soup back to the boil, and simmer for 1 minute.

4 Adjust the seasoning and serve the soup hot, garnished with the spring onions (scallions).

COOKING TIPS

Soups such as this are improved enormously in flavour if you use a well-flavoured stock. Either use a stock cube, or find time to make Chinese Stock – see the recipe on page 230. Better still, make double quantities and freeze some for future use.

Fresh, uncooked prawns (shrimp) impart the best flavour. If these are not available, you can use ready-cooked prawns (shrimp). They must be added at the last moment before serving to prevent them becoming tough and over-cooked.

STEP 1

STEP 2

STEP 3

STEP 4

PORK & SZECHUAN VEGETABLE

Sold in cans, Szechuan preserved vegetable is pickled mustard root which is quite hot and salty, so rinse in water before use.

SERVES 4

250 g/8 oz pork fillet (tenderloin)
2 tsp cornflour (cornstarch) paste
  (see page 231)
125 g/4 oz Szechuan preserved vegetable
750 ml/1¼ pints/3 cups Chinese stock
  (see page 230) or water
salt and pepper
a few drops sesame oil (optional)
2–3 spring onions (scallions), sliced, to
  garnish

1 Cut the pork across the grain into thin shreds and mix with the cornflour (cornstarch) paste.

2 Wash and rinse the Szechuan preserved vegetable, then cut into thin shreds the same size as the pork.

3 Bring the stock or water to a rolling boil. Add the pork and stir to separate the shreds. Return to the boil.

4 Add the Szechuan preserved vegetable and bring back to the boil once more. Adjust the seasoning and sprinkle with sesame oil. Serve hot, garnished with spring onions (scallions).

SZECHUAN PRESERVED VEGETABLE

The Chinese are fond of pickles, and there are many varieties of pickled vegetables. In the Szechuan region, in particular, preserved vegetables are important because the region is over 1,600 km (1,000 miles) from the coast. Vinegar and salt (from the province's extensive salt mines) are used to make a range of pickled foods, which are used in cooking and eaten on their own.

One of the most popular is Szechuan preserved vegetable, a speciality of the province, available in cans from specialist Chinese supermarkets. It is actually mustard green root, pickled in salt and chillies. It gives a crunchy, spicy taste to dishes. Rinse in cold water before use. Once opened the vegetable should be stored in a tightly sealed jar and kept in the refrigerator.

STEP 1

SPINACH & TOFU (BEAN CURD) SOUP

This is a very colourful and delicious soup. If spinach is not in season, watercress or lettuce can be used instead.

STEP 1

SERVES 4

1 cake tofu (bean curd)
125 g/4 oz spinach leaves without stalks
  (stems)
750 ml/1¼ pints/3 cups Chinese Stock
  (see page 230) or water
1 tbsp light soy sauce
salt and pepper

1 Cut the tofu (bean curd) into small pieces about 5 mm (¼ inch) thick. Wash the spinach leaves and cut them into small pieces or shreds, discarding any discoloured leaves and tough stalks (stems). (If possible, use fresh young spinach leaves, which have not yet developed tough ribs. Otherwise, it is important to cut out all the ribs and stems for this soup.)

2 In a wok or large pan, bring the stock to a rolling boil. Add the tofu and soy sauce, bring back to the boil and simmer for about 2 minutes.

3 Add the spinach and simmer for 1 more minute.

4 Skim the surface of the soup to make it clear, adjust the seasoning and serve.

STEP 2

STEP 3

> ## SERVING SUGGESTIONS
>
> There is no set order of courses for Chinese meals. The soup is an integral part of the meal; it may be served first, but people can help themselves to more during the meal. The soup is usually presented in a large bowl placed in the centre of the table, and consumed as the meal progresses. It serves as a refresher between different dishes and as a beverage throughout the meal. (Water is never served during the meal, and tea is brought only before and after a meal.)
>
> Each person at the table has a bowl, rather than a plate, that is used for all dishes. Chopsticks are used for picking up the food – or in the case of soups, a broad, shallow spoon.

CHAPTER THIRTEEN

Seafood Dishes

As in the rest of China, Szechuan food features fish in many dishes, especially freshwater fish from the mighty Yangtze river, which flows through the region.

Szechuan dishes are noted for their hot, spicy character, and fish and seafood dishes are no exception. Whole fish, and fish fillets, are served in thick, spicy sauces, as in Braised Fish Fillets (see page 187). Prawn (shrimp) dishes are equally hot and spicy, with garlic, ginger and chilli appearing in almost every recipe – Szechuan Prawns (Shrimp) (see page 183) is a typical example.

Opposite: The Yangtze river near Guilin. Until recently the Yangtze was Szechuan's main avenue of communication with the rest of China.

STEP 2

STEP 3

STEP 3

STEP 4

SWEET & SOUR PRAWNS (SHRIMP) WITH WATER CHESTNUTS

Use raw prawns (shrimp) if possible. Omit steps 1 and 2 if ready-cooked ones are used.

SERVES 4

175–250 g/6–8 oz peeled raw tiger prawns
  (or jumbo shrimp)
pinch salt
1 tsp egg white
1 tsp cornflour (cornstarch) paste (see
  page 231)
300 ml/¹/₂ pint/1¹/₄ cups vegetable oil

SAUCE:
1 tbsp vegetable oil
¹/₂ small green (bell) pepper, cored, deseeded
  and thinly sliced
¹/₂ small carrot, thinly sliced
125 g/4 oz canned water chestnuts, rinsed,
  drained and sliced
¹/₂ tsp salt
1 tbsp light soy sauce
2 tbsp sugar
3 tbsp rice or sherry vinegar
1 tsp rice wine or dry sherry
1 tbsp tomato sauce
¹/₂ tsp chilli sauce
3–4 tbsp Chinese Stock (see page 230) or
  water
2 tsp cornflour (cornstarch) paste (see
  page 231)
a few drops sesame oil

1 Mix the prawns (shrimp) with the salt, egg white and cornflour (cornstarch) paste.

2 Heat the oil in a preheated wok and stir-fry the prawns (shrimp) for 30–40 seconds only. Remove and drain on paper towels.

3 Pour off the oil and wipe the wok clean with paper towels. To make the sauce, first heat the tablespoon of oil. Add the vegetables and stir-fry for about 1 minute, then add the seasonings with the stock or water and bring to the boil.

4 Add the prawns (shrimp) and stir until blended well. Thicken the sauce with the cornflour (cornstarch) paste and stir until smooth. Sprinkle with sesame oil and serve hot.

SESAME OIL

Sesame oil has a distinctive nutty flavour and aroma. It is widely used in China as a seasoning and is usually sprinkled on at the last moment, to finish a dish. It is now widely available in supermarkets. Use sparingly.

SZECHUAN PRAWNS (SHRIMP)

Raw prawns (shrimp) should be used if possible, otherwise omit steps 1 and 2 and add cooked prawns (shrimp) before the sauce ingredients at the beginning of step 3.

STEP 1

SERVES 4

250–300 g/8–10 oz raw tiger prawns (or jumbo shrimp)
pinch salt
1/2 egg white, lightly beaten
1 tsp cornflour (cornstarch) paste (see page 231)
600 ml/1pint/2 1/2 cups vegetable oil
fresh coriander (cilantro) leaves, to garnish

SAUCE:
1 tsp finely chopped ginger root
2 spring onions (scallions), finely chopped
1 garlic clove, finely chopped
3–4 small dried red chillies, deseeded and chopped
1 tbsp light soy sauce
1 tsp rice wine or dry sherry
1 tbsp tomato purée (paste)
1 tbsp oyster sauce
2–3 tbsp Chinese Stock (see page 230) or water
a few drops sesame oil

1 Peel the raw prawns (shrimp), then mix with the salt, egg white and cornflour (cornstarch) paste until well coated.

2 Heat the oil in a preheated wok until it is smoking. Deep-fry the prawns (shrimp) in hot oil for about 1 minute. Remove with a slotted spoon and drain on paper towels.

3 Pour off the oil, leaving about 1 tablespoon in the wok. Add all the ingredients for the sauce, bring to the boil and stir until smooth and well blended.

4 Add the prawns (shrimp) to the sauce and stir until blended well. Serve garnished with fresh coriander (cilantro) leaves.

STEP 2

STEP 3

CHILLIES

In Szechuan dishes chillies are often left unseeded, giving an extremely hot flavour to dishes. If you dislike very hot food, make sure the dried chillies are carefully seeded before use.

STEP 4

STEP 1

STEP 2

STEP 3

STEP 4

SZECHUAN STIR-FRIED PRAWNS (SHRIMP)

The (bell) peppers in this dish can be replaced by either mangetout (snow peas) or broccoli – the idea is to contrast the pinky/orange prawns (shrimp) with a bright green vegetable.

SERVES 4

175g/6 oz raw prawns (shrimp), peeled
1 tsp salt
¼ tsp egg white
2 tsp cornflour (cornstarch) paste (see page 231)
300 ml/½ pint/1¼ cups vegetable oil
1 spring onion (scallion), cut into short sections
2.5 cm (1 inch) ginger root, thinly sliced
1 small green (bell) pepper, cored, deseeded and cubed
½ tsp sugar
1 tbsp light soy sauce
1 tsp rice wine or dry sherry
a few drops sesame oil

1 Mix the prawns (shrimp) with a pinch of the salt, the egg white and cornflour (cornstarch) paste until they are all well coated.

2 Heat the oil in a preheated wok and stir-fry the prawns (shrimp) for 30–40 seconds only. Remove and drain on paper towels.

3 Pour off the oil, leaving about 1 tablespoon in the wok. Add the spring onion (scallion) and ginger to flavour the oil for a few seconds, then add

the green (bell) pepper and stir-fry for about 1 minute.

4 Add the remaining salt and the sugar followed by the prawns (shrimp). Continue stirring for another minute or so, then add the soy sauce and wine and blend well. Sprinkle with sesame oil and serve immediately.

COOK'S HINTS

One or 2 small green or red hot chillies, sliced, can be added with the green (bell) pepper to create a more spicy dish. Leave the chillies unseeded for a very hot dish.

Fresh ginger root, sold by weight, should be peeled and sliced, then finely chopped or shredded before use. It will keep for weeks in a cool, dry place. Dried ginger powder is no substitute. In comparison with fresh ginger root, it is lacking in flavour.

BRAISED FISH FILLETS

Any white fish such as lemon sole or plaice (flounder) is ideal for this dish.

STEP 2

SERVES 4

3–4 small Chinese dried mushrooms
300–350 g/10–12 oz fish fillets
1 tsp salt
½ egg white, lightly beaten
1 tsp cornflour (cornstarch) paste (see
    page 231)
600 ml/1 pint/2½ cups vegetable oil
1 tsp finely chopped ginger root
2 spring onions (scallions), finely chopped
1 garlic clove, finely chopped
½ small green (bell) pepper, cored, deseeded
    and cut into small cubes
½ small carrot, thinly sliced
60 g/2 oz canned sliced bamboo shoots,
    rinsed and drained
½ tsp sugar
1 tbsp light soy sauce
1 tsp rice wine or dry sherry
1 tbsp chilli bean sauce
2–3 tbsp Chinese Stock (see page 230) or
    water
a few drops sesame oil

1 Soak the Chinese mushrooms in warm water for 30 minutes, then drain on paper towels, reserving the soaking water for stock or soup. Squeeze the mushrooms to extract all the moisture, cut off and discard any hard stems and slice thinly.

2 Cut the fish into bite-sized pieces, then place in a shallow dish and mix with a pinch of salt, the egg white and cornflour (cornstarch) paste, turning the fish to coat well.

3 Heat the oil and deep-fry the fish pieces for about 1 minute. Remove with a slotted spoon and drain on paper towels.

4 Pour off the oil, leaving about 1 tablespoon in the wok. Add the ginger, spring onions (scallions) and garlic to flavour the oil for a few seconds, then add the vegetables and stir-fry for about 1 minute.

5 Add the salt, sugar, soy sauce, wine, chilli bean sauce and stock or water and bring to the boil. Add the fish pieces, stir to coat well with the sauce, and braise for another minute. Sprinkle with sesame oil and serve immediately.

STEP 3

STEP 4

STEP 5

FISH IN SZECHUAN HOT SAUCE

*This is a classic Szechuan recipe. When served in a restaurant, the fish
head and tail are removed before cooking.*

STEP 1

STEP 2

STEP 3

STEP 3

SERVES 4

1 carp, bream, sea bass, trout, grouper or
  grey mullet, about 750 g/1¹/₂ lb, gutted
1 tbsp light soy sauce
1 tbsp Chinese rice wine or dry sherry
vegetable oil for deep-frying
flat-leaf parsley or coriander (cilantro)
  sprigs, to garnish

SAUCE:
2 garlic cloves, finely chopped
2–3 spring onions (scallions), finely chopped
1 tsp finely chopped ginger root
2 tbsp chilli bean sauce
1 tbsp tomato purée (paste)
2 tsp sugar
1 tbsp rice vinegar
125 ml/4 fl oz/¹/₂ cup Chinese Stock (see
  page 230) or water
1 tbsp cornflour (cornstarch) paste (see
  page 231)
¹/₂ tsp sesame oil

1 Wash the fish and dry well on
paper towels. Score both sides of
the fish to the bone with a sharp knife,
making diagonal cuts at intervals of
about 2.5 cm/1 inch. Rub the fish with
the soy sauce and wine on both sides,
then leave on a plate in the refrigerator
to marinate for 10–15 minutes.

2 Heat the oil in a preheated wok
until smoking. Deep-fry the fish in
the hot oil for 3–4 minutes on both sides,
or until golden brown.

3 Pour off the oil, leaving about 1
tablespoon in the wok. Push the
fish to one side of the wok and add the
garlic, white parts of the spring onions
(scallions), ginger, chilli bean sauce,
tomato purée (paste), sugar, vinegar and
stock. Bring to the boil and braise the fish
in the sauce for 4–5 minutes, turning it
over once.

4 Add the green parts of the spring
onions (scallions) and stir in the
cornflour (cornstarch) paste to thicken
the sauce. Sprinkle with sesame oil and
serve immediately, garnished with
parsley or coriander (cilantro).

CHAPTER FOURTEEN

Meat & Poultry Dishes

Poultry is popular in Szechuan as elsewhere in China, though characteristically it is much hotter and spicier than elsewhere – Chilli Chicken (see page 197) is a typical example.

Beef appears on the menu more often than in the South or East. A favourite form of cooking is stir-frying, giving a dry, chewy texture. Braising and steaming are also popular methods of cooking beef and pork, ensuring a tender result, and so too is double-cooking. This is a technique in which the meat is first tenderized by long, slow simmering in water, followed by a quick crisping or stir-frying in a sauce – Twice-cooked Pork (see page 203) is a delicious example of this technique.

Opposite: *The fertile soil of Szechuan produces abundant crops almost all the year round.*

STEP 1

STEP 2

STEP 2

STEP 4

AROMATIC & CRISPY DUCK

Although the pancakes traditionally served with this dish are not too difficult to make, the process is very time-consuming. Buy ready-made ones from Oriental stores, or use crisp lettuce leaves as the wrapper.

SERVES 4

2 large duckling quarters
1 tsp salt
3–4 pieces star anise
1 tsp Szechuan red peppercorns
1 tsp cloves
2 cinnamon sticks, broken into pieces
2–3 spring onions (scallions), cut into short
   sections
4–5 small slices ginger root
3–4 tbsp rice wine or dry sherry
vegetable oil for deep-frying

TO SERVE:
12 ready-made pancakes or 12 crisp lettuce
   leaves
hoi-sin or plum sauce
1/4 cucumber, thinly shredded
3–4 spring onions (scallions), thinly
   shredded

1 Rub the duck pieces with the salt and arrange the star anise, peppercorns, cloves and cinnamon on top. Sprinkle with the spring onions (scallions), ginger and wine and leave to marinate for at least 3–4 hours.

2 Arrange the duck pieces (with the marinade spices) on a plate that will fit inside a bamboo steamer. Pour some hot water into a wok, place the bamboo steamer in the wok, sitting on a trivet. Put in the duck and cover with the bamboo lid. Steam the duck pieces (with the marinade) over high heat for at least 2–3 hours, until tender and cooked through. Top up the hot water from time to time as required.

3 Remove the duck and leave to cool for at least 4–5 hours – this is very important, for unless the duck is cold and dry, it will not be crispy.

4 Pour off the water and wipe the wok dry. Pour in the oil and heat until smoking. Deep-fry the duck pieces, skin-side down, for 4–5 minutes or until crisp and brown. Remove and drain on paper towels.

5 To serve, scrape the meat off the bone, place about 1 teaspoon of hoi-sin or plum sauce on the centre of a pancake (or lettuce leaf), add a few pieces of cucumber and spring onion (scallion) with a portion of the duck meat. Wrap up to form a small parcel and eat with your fingers. Provide plenty of paper napkins for your guests.

STEP 1

STEP 2

STEP 3

STEP 4

KUNG PO CHICKEN WITH CASHEW NUTS

Peanuts, walnuts or almonds can be used instead of the cashew nuts, if preferred.

SERVES 4

250–300 g/8–10 oz boneless chicken
  meat, skinned
¼ tsp salt
⅓ egg white
1 tsp cornflour (cornstarch) paste (see
  page 231)
1 medium green (bell) pepper, cored and
  deseeded
4 tbsp vegetable oil
1 spring onion (scallion), cut into short
  sections
a few small ginger root slices
4–5 small dried red chillies, soaked, deseeded
  and shredded
2 tbsp crushed yellow bean sauce
1 tsp rice wine or dry sherry
125 g/4 oz/1 cup roasted cashew nuts
a few drops sesame oil
boiled rice, to serve

1 Cut the chicken into small cubes about the size of sugar lumps. Place the chicken in a small bowl and mix with a pinch of salt, the egg white and the cornflour (cornstarch) paste, in that order.

2 Cut the green (bell) pepper into cubes or triangles about the same size as the chicken pieces.

3 Heat the oil in a preheated wok. Add the chicken cubes and stir-fry for about 1 minute, or until the colour changes. Remove with a slotted spoon and keep warm.

4 Add the spring onion (scallion), ginger, chillies and green (bell) pepper. Stir-fry for about 1 minute, then add the chicken with the yellow bean sauce and wine. Blend well and stir-fry for another minute. Finally stir in the cashew nuts and sesame oil. Serve hot.

VARIATIONS

Any nuts can be used in place of the cashew nuts, if preferred. The important point is the crunchy texture, which is very much a feature of Szechuan cooking.

SZECHUAN CHILLI CHICKEN

*In China, the chicken pieces are chopped through the bone for this dish,
but if you do not possess a cleaver, use filleted chicken meat.*

STEP 1

SERVES 4

500 g/ 1 lb chicken thighs
1/4 tsp pepper
1 tbsp sugar
2 tsp light soy sauce
1 tsp dark soy sauce
1 tbsp rice wine or dry sherry
2 tsp cornflour (cornstarch)
2–3 tbsp vegetable oil
1–2 garlic cloves, crushed
2 spring onions (scallions), cut into short
    sections, with the green and white parts
    separated
4–6 small dried red chillies, soaked and
    deseeded
2 tbsp crushed yellow bean sauce
about 150 ml/1/4 pint/2/3 cup Chinese Stock
    (see page 230) or water

1 Cut or chop the chicken thighs
into bite-sized pieces and marinate
with the pepper, sugar, soy sauce,
wine and cornflour (cornstarch) for
25–30 minutes.

2 Heat the oil in a preheated wok.
Add the chicken pieces and stir-fry
until lightly brown for about 1–2
minutes. Remove the chicken pieces with
a slotted spoon, remove to a warm dish
and reserve.

3 Add the garlic, the white parts of
the spring onions (scallions), the
chillies and yellow bean sauce to the wok
and stir-fry for about 30 seconds,
blending well.

4 Return the chicken pieces to the
wok, stirring constantly for 1–2
minutes, then add the stock or water,
bring to the boil and cover. Braise over
medium heat for 5–6 minutes, stirring
once or twice. Garnish with the green
parts of the spring onions (scallions) and
serve immediately.

STEP 2

STEP 3

CHILLIES

One of the striking features of Szechuan
cooking is the quantity of chillies used.
Food generally in this region is much
hotter than elsewhere in China – people
tend to keep a string of dry chillies
hanging from the eaves of their houses.

STEP 4

STEP 1

STEP 2

STEP 3

STEP 4

CHICKEN WITH (BELL) PEPPERS

*Red (bell) pepper or celery can also be used in this recipe;
the method is the same.*

SERVES 4

*300 g/10 oz boned, skinned chicken breast
1 tsp salt
¹/₂ egg white
2 tsp cornflour (cornstarch) paste (see
    page 231)
1 medium green (bell) pepper, cored and
    deseeded
300 ml/¹/₂ pint/1¹/₄ cups vegetable oil
1 spring onion (scallion), finely shredded
a few strips ginger root, thinly shredded
1–2 red chillies, deseeded and thinly
    shredded
¹/₂ tsp sugar
1 tbsp rice wine or dry sherry
a few drops sesame oil*

1 Cut the chicken breast into strips,
then mix in a bowl with a pinch of
the salt, the egg white and cornflour
(cornstarch), in that order.

2 Cut the green (bell) pepper into thin
shreds the same size and length as
the chicken strips.

3 Heat the oil in a preheated wok.
Add the chicken strips and deep-fry
them in batches for about 1 minute, or
until the colour of the chicken changes.
Remove the chicken strips with a slotted

spoon and keep warm while you
complete the recipe.

4 Pour off the excess oil from the
wok, leaving about 1 tablespoon.
Add the spring onion (scallion), ginger,
chillies and green (bell) pepper. Stir-fry
for about 1 minute, then return the
chicken to the wok together with the
remaining salt, the sugar and wine. Stir-
fry for another minute, sprinkle with
sesame oil and serve.

RICE WINE

Rice wine is used everywhere in China for
both cooking and drinking. Made from
glutinous rice, it is known as "yellow
wine" (Huang jiu or chiew in Chinese)
because of its rich amber colour. The
best variety is called Shao Hsing or Shaoxing,
and comes from the south-east of China.
Rice wine is more powerful than wines in
the West – about 16° proof – and sherry is
the best substitute as a cooking
ingredient.

STEP 1

STEP 1

STEP 3

STEP 4

FISH-FLAVOURED SHREDDED PORK

'Fish-flavoured' (yu-xiang in Chinese) is a Szechuan cookery term meaning that the dish is prepared with seasonings normally used in fish dishes.

SERVES 4

about 2 tbsp dried wood ears
250–300 g/8–10 oz pork fillet (tenderloin)
1 tsp salt
2 tsp cornflour (cornstarch) paste (see page 231)
3 tbsp vegetable oil
1 garlic clove, finely chopped
1/2 tsp finely chopped ginger root
2 spring onions (scallions), finely chopped, with the white and green parts separated
2 celery sticks, thinly sliced
1/2 tsp sugar
1 tbsp light soy sauce
1 tbsp chilli bean sauce
2 tsp rice vinegar
1 tsp rice wine or dry sherry
a few drops sesame oil

1 Soak the wood ears in warm water for about 20 minutes, then rinse in cold water until the water is clear. Drain well, then cut into thin shreds.

2 Cut the pork into thin shreds, then mix in a bowl with a pinch of salt and about half the cornflour (cornstarch) paste until well coated.

3 Heat 1 tablespoon of oil in a preheated wok. Add the pork strips and stir-fry for about 1 minute, or until the colour changes, then remove with a slotted spoon.

4 Add the remaining oil to the wok and heat. Add the garlic, ginger, the white parts of the spring onions (scallions), the wood ears and celery. Stir-fry for about 1 minute, then return the pork strips together with the salt, sugar, soy sauce, chilli bean sauce, vinegar and wine. Blend well and continue stirring for another minute.

5 Finally add the green parts of the spring onions (scallions) and blend in the remaining cornflour (cornstarch) paste and sesame oil. Stir until the sauce has thickened and serve hot.

DRIED WOOD EARS

Also known as cloud ears, this is a dried grey-black fungus widely used in Szechuan cooking. It is always soaked in warm water before using. Wood ears have a crunchy texture and a mild flavour.

TWICE-COOKED PORK

Twice-cooked is a popular way of cooking meat in China. The meat is first boiled to tenderize it, then cut into strips or slices and stir-fried.

STEP 1

SERVES 4

250–300 g/8–10 oz shoulder or leg of pork, in one piece
1 small green (bell) pepper, cored and deseeded
1 small red (bell) pepper, cored and deseeded
125 g/4 oz canned sliced bamboo shoots, rinsed and drained
3 tbsp vegetable oil
1 spring onion (scallion), cut into short sections
1 tsp salt
¹/₂ tsp sugar
1 tbsp light soy sauce
1 tsp chilli bean sauce or very finely chopped (minced) fresh chilli
1 tsp rice wine or dry sherry
a few drops sesame oil

1 Immerse the pork in a pot of boiling water to cover. Return to the boil and skim the surface. Reduce the heat, cover and simmer for 15–20 minutes. Turn off the heat and leave the pork in the water to cool for 2–3 hours.

2 Remove the pork from the water and drain well. Trim off any excess fat, then cut into small, thin slices. Cut the green and red (bell) peppers into pieces about the same size as the pork

STEP 1

and the sliced bamboo shoots.

3 Heat the oil in a preheated wok. Add the vegetables together with the spring onion (scallion). Stir-fry for about 1 minute.

4 Add the pork, followed by the salt, sugar, soy sauce, chilli bean sauce and wine. Blend well, continue stirring for another minute, then sprinkle with sesame oil and serve.

STEP 2

PREPARING THE MEAT

For ease of handling, buy a boned piece of meat, and roll into a compact shape. Tie securely with string before placing in the boiling water.

STEP 4

STEP 1

STEP 2

STEP 3

STEP 4

CRISPY SHREDDED BEEF

A very popular Szechuan dish served in most Chinese restaurants all over the world.

SERVES 4

300–350 g/10–12 oz beef steak, such as topside or rump (sirloin)
2 eggs
¼ tsp salt
4–5 tbsp plain (all-purpose) flour
vegetable oil for deep-frying
2 carrots, finely shredded
2 spring onions (scallions), thinly shredded
1 garlic clove, finely chopped
2–3 small fresh green or red chillies, deseeded and thinly shredded
4 tbsp sugar
3 tbsp rice vinegar
1 tbsp light soy sauce
2–3 tbsp Chinese Stock (see page 230) or water
1 tsp cornflour (cornstarch) paste (see page 231)

1 Cut the steak across the grain into thin strips. Beat the eggs in a bowl with the salt and flour, adding a little water if necessary. Add the beef strips and mix well until coated with the batter.

2 Heat the oil in a preheated wok until smoking. Add the beef strips and deep-fry for 4–5 minutes, stirring to separate the shreds. Remove with a slotted spoon and drain on paper towels.

3 Add the carrots to the wok and deep-fry for about 1–1½ minutes, then remove with a slotted spoon and drain on paper towels.

4 Pour off the excess oil, leaving about 1 tablespoon in the wok. Add the spring onions (scallions), garlic, chillies and carrots and stir-fry for about 1 minute, then add the sugar, vinegar, soy sauce and stock or water, blend well and bring to the boil.

5 Stir in the cornflour (cornstarch) paste and simmer for a few minutes to thicken the sauce. Return the beef to the wok and stir until the shreds of meat are well coated with the sauce. Serve hot.

TEXTURES

This dish is typical of the chewy-textured food that is so popular in Szechuan. Unlike dishes in Eastern China many Szechuan dishes are fried with only the minimum of sauce to convey the seasonings: the sauce itself is not an important element in the dish as in Canton.

BEEF & CHILLI BLACK BEAN SAUCE

It is not necessary to use the expensive cuts of beef steak for this recipe: the meat will be tender as it is cut into small thin slices and marinated.

STEP 1

SERVES 4

250–300 g/8–10 oz beef steak, such as
   rump
1 small onion
1 small green (bell) pepper, cored and
   deseeded
about 300 ml/¹/₂ pint/1¹/₄ cups vegetable oil
1 spring onion (scallion), cut into short
   sections
a few small ginger root slices
1–2 small green or red chillies, deseeded and
   sliced
2 tbsp crushed black bean sauce

MARINADE:
¹/₂ tsp bicarbonate of soda or baking powder
¹/₂ tsp sugar
1 tbsp light soy sauce
2 tsp rice wine or dry sherry
2 tsp cornflour (cornstarch) paste (see
   page 231)
2 tsp sesame oil

1 Cut the beef into small thin strips. Mix together the marinade ingredients in a shallow dish, add the beef strips, turn to coat and leave to marinate for at least 2–3 hours – the longer the better.

2 Cut the onion and green (bell) pepper into small cubes.

3 Heat the oil in a preheated wok. Add the beef strips and stir-fry for about 1 minute, or until the colour changes. Remove with a slotted spoon and drain on paper towels. Keep warm.

4 Pour off the excess oil, leaving about 1 tablespoon in the wok. Add the spring onion (scallion), ginger, chillies, onion and green (bell) pepper and stir-fry for about 1 minute. Add the black bean sauce, stir until smooth then return the beef strips to the wok. Blend well and stir-fry for another minute. Serve hot.

STEP 2

STEP 3

MARINADES

Do make sure that you marinade the beef for the time specified – it will then be wonderfully soft and tender.

STEP 4

CHAPTER FIFTEEN

Vegetables, Rice & Noodles

With its fertile soil and warm humid climate, Szechuan is
one of the most prosperous regions of China, and crops can
be grown almost all year round. Fruit, vegetables and cereal
crops grow in abundance, as well as mushrooms and fungi.
Pickling, drying and salting techniques are used extensively to help
preserve this abundance of food – partly because the humid climate
makes it difficult to keep food fresh.

As with other dishes, these tend to be highly spiced, and are
usually on the hot side. 'Fish-flavoured', as in the aubergine
(eggplant) dish on page 215, sounds strange, but is a popular
way of describing dishes cooked with a variety of spices and
flavourings – it has nothing to do with fish, and
tastes delicious!

Opposite: *Rice plants hanging
up to dry on bamboo racks. Rice
is a staple crop in China and the
fertile soil of Szechuan produces
vast quantities of it.*

STEP 1

STEP 2

STEP 3

STEP 4

MA-PO TOFU (BEAN CURD)

Ma-Po was the wife of a Szechuan chef who created this popular dish in the middle of the 19th century. The beef can be replaced by Chinese dried mushrooms to make a vegetarian meal.

SERVES 4

3 cakes tofu (bean curd)
3 tbsp vegetable oil
125 g/4 oz coarsely minced (ground) beef
½ tsp finely chopped garlic
1 leek, cut into short sections
½ tsp salt
1 tbsp black bean sauce
1 tbsp light soy sauce
1 tsp chilli bean sauce
3–4 tbsp Chinese Stock (see page 230) or water
2 tsp cornflour (cornstarch) paste (see page 231)
a few drops sesame oil
black pepper
finely chopped spring onions (scallions), to garnish

1 Cut the tofu (bean curd) into 1 cm/ ½ inch cubes, handling it carefully. Bring some water to the boil in a small pan or a wok, add the tofu (bean curd) and blanch for 2–3 minutes to harden. Remove and drain well.

2 Heat the oil in a preheated wok. Add the minced (ground) beef and garlic and stir-fry for about 1 minute, or until the colour of the beef changes. Add the chopped leek, salt and sauces and

continue stir-frying until all the ingredients are well blended.

3 Add the stock or water followed by the tofu (bean curd). Bring to the boil and braise gently for 2–3 minutes.

4 Add the cornflour (cornstarch) paste, and stir until the sauce has thickened. Sprinkle with sesame oil and black pepper and garnish with spring onions (scallions). Serve hot.

TOFU (BEAN CURD)

Tofu (bean curd) has been an important element in Chinese cooking for more than 1,000 years. It is made of yellow soya beans, which are soaked, ground and mixed with water. Tofu (bean curd) is highly nutritious, being rich in protein, and has a very bland taste. Solid cakes of tofu (bean curd) can be cut up with a sharp knife. Cook carefully as too much stirring can cause it to disintegrate.

STEP 1

STEP 1

STEP 3

STEP 4

BRAISED TOFU (BEAN CURD), HOME STYLE

The pork used in the recipe can be replaced by chicken or prawns (shrimps), or it can be omitted altogether.

SERVES 4

3 cakes tofu (bean curd)
125 g/4 oz boneless pork (or any other type of meat)
1 leek
1–2 spring onions (scallions), cut into short sections
a few small dried whole chillies, soaked
vegetable oil for deep-frying
2 tbsp crushed yellow bean sauce
1 tbsp light soy sauce
2 tsp rice wine or dry sherry
a few drops sesame oil

1 Split each tofu (bean curd) cake into 3 slices crosswise, then cut each slice diagonally into 2 triangles.

2 Cut the pork into small thin slices or shreds; cut the leek into thin strips. Drain the chillies, remove the seeds using the tip of a knife, then cut into small shreds.

3 Heat the oil in a preheated wok until smoking. Deep-fry the tofu triangles for 2–3 minutes or until golden brown all over. Remove with a slotted spoon and drain on paper towels.

4 Pour off the hot oil, leaving about 1 tablespoon in the wok. Add the pork strips, spring onions (scallions) and chillies and stir-fry for about 1 minute or until the pork changes colour.

5 Add the leek, tofu (bean curd), yellow bean sauce, soy sauce and wine and braise for 2–3 minutes, stirring very gently to blend everything well. Finally sprinkle on the sesame oil and serve.

BRAISED TOFU (BEAN CURD)

Tofu (bean curd) is sold in 2 forms: as firm cakes, or as a thickish junket, known as silken tofu (bean curd). It is the solid kind that is used for braising and stir-frying. Silken tofu (bean curd) is usually added to soups or sauces. It is also possible to buy dried tofu (bean curd) and smoked tofu (bean curd) in specialist Oriental stores. It is acceptable to store tofu (bean curd) for a few days if it is submerged in water in an air-tight container, then placed in the refrigerator.

FISH AUBERGINE (EGGPLANT)

Like Fish-flavoured Shredded Pork (see page 200), there is no fish involved in this dish, and the meat can be omitted without affecting the flavour.

STEP 1

SERVES 4

500 g/1 lb aubergine (eggplant)
vegetable oil for deep-frying
1 garlic clove, finely chopped
½ tsp finely chopped ginger root
2 spring onions (scallions), finely chopped,
    with the white and green parts separated
125 g/4 oz pork fillet (tenderloin), thinly
    shredded (optional)
1 tbsp light soy sauce
2 tsp rice wine or dry sherry
1 tbsp chilli bean sauce
½ tsp salt
½ tsp sugar
1 tbsp rice vinegar
2 tsp cornflour (cornstarch) paste (see
    page 231)
a few drops sesame oil

1 Cut the aubergine (eggplant) into rounds and then into thin strips about the size of potato chips (French fries)– the skin can be peeled or left on.

2 Heat the oil in a preheated wok until smoking. Add the aubergine (eggplant) chips (fries) and deep-fry for 3–4 minutes, or until soft. Remove and drain on paper towels.

3 Pour off the hot oil, leaving about 1 tablespoon in the wok. Add the garlic, ginger and the white parts of the spring onions (scallions), followed by the pork (if using). Stir-fry for about 1 minute or until the colour of the meat changes, then add the soy sauce, wine and chilli bean sauce, blending them in well.

4 Return the aubergine (eggplant) chips (fries) to the wok together with the salt, sugar and vinegar. Continue stirring for another minute or so, then add the cornflour (cornstarch) paste and stir until the sauce has thickened.

5 Add the green parts of the spring onions (scallions) to the wok and sprinkle on the sesame oil. Serve hot.

STEP 2

STEP 3

FISH-FLAVOURED DISHES

These multiple-flavoured dishes, using garlic, chilli sauce, vinegar, sugar and soy sauce all together, are always described as 'fish-flavoured', although there is no fish in the recipe. These dishes are only found in Szechuan.

STEP 4

STIR-FRIED SEASONAL VEGETABLES

When selecting different fresh vegetables for this dish, bear in mind that there should always be a contrast in colour as well as texture.

STEP 1

STEP 2

STEP 3

STEP 4

SERVES 4

1 medium red (bell) pepper, cored and
  deseeded
125g/4 oz courgettes (zucchini)
125g/4 oz cauliflower
125g/4 oz French beans
3 tbsp vegetable oil
a few small ginger root slices
1/2 tsp salt
1/2 tsp sugar
Chinese Stock (see page 230) or water
1 tbsp light soy sauce
a few drops sesame oil (optional)

1 Cut the red (bell) pepper into small squares. Thinly slice the courgettes (zucchini). Trim the cauliflower and divide into small florets, discarding any thick stems (stalks). Make sure the vegetables are cut into roughly similar shapes and sizes to ensure even cooking.

2 Top and tail the French beans, then cut them in half.

3 Heat the oil in a pre-heated wok. Add the vegetables and stir-fry with the ginger for about 2 minutes.

4 Add the salt and sugar to the wok, and continue to stir-fry for 1–2

minutes, adding a little Chinese stock or water if the vegetables appear to be too dry. Do not add liquid unless it seems necessary.

5 Add the light soy sauce and sesame oil (if using) blend well to lightly coat the vegetables and serve at once.

VEGETABLES

Almost any vegetables could be used in this dish: other good choices would be mangetout (snow peas), broccoli florets, carrots, baby corn cobs, green peas, Chinese cabbage and young spinach leaves. Either white or black (oyster) mushrooms can also be used to give a greater diversity of textures. Make sure there is a good variety of colour, and always include several crisp vegetables such as carrots or mangetout (snow peas).

STEP 1

STEP 2

STEP 3

STEP 4

BRAISED CHINESE LEAVES

White cabbage can be used instead of the Chinese leaves for this dish.

SERVES 4

500 g/ 1 lb Chinese leaves or white cabbage
3 tbsp vegetable oil
½ tsp Szechuan red peppercorns
5–6 small dried red chillies, deseeded and
   chopped
½ tsp salt
1 tbsp sugar
1 tbsp light soy sauce
1 tbsp rice vinegar
a few drops sesame oil (optional)

1 Shred the Chinese leaves or cabbage crosswise into thin pieces. (If Chinese leaves are unavailable, the best alternative to use in this recipe is a firm-packed white cabbage; not the dark green type of cabbage. Cut out the thick core of the cabbage with a sharp knife before shredding.)

2 Heat the oil in a pre-heated wok. Add the Szechuan red peppercorns and dried red chillies and stir for a few seconds.

3 Add the Chinese leaves or shredded cabbage to the peppercorns and chillies, stir-fry for about 1 minute, then add salt and continue stirring for another minute.

4 Add the sugar, soy sauce and vinegar, blend well and braise for 1 more minute. Finally sprinkle on the sesame oil, if using. Serve hot or cold.

PEPPERCORNS

It is important to use the correct type of peppercorns in preparing this dish. Szechuan red peppercorns are also known as farchiew. They are not true peppers, but reddish brown dry berries with a pungent, aromatic odour which distinguishes them from the hotter black peppercorns. Roast them briefly in the oven or sauté them in a dry frying pan (skillet). Grind the peppercorns in a blender and store in a jar until needed.

STEP 1

STEP 2

STEP 3

STEP 4

CHICKEN OR PORK CHOW MEIN

This is a basic recipe – the meat and/or vegetables can be varied as much as you like.

SERVES 4

250 g/8 oz Chinese egg noodles
4–5 tbsp vegetable oil
125g/4 oz French beans
250 g/8 oz chicken breast meat, or pork fillet (tenderloin), cooked
2 tbsp light soy sauce
1 tsp salt
¹/₂ tsp sugar
1 tbsp Chinese rice wine or dry sherry
2 spring onions (scallions), finely shredded
a few drops sesame oil
chilli sauce, to serve (optional)

1 Cook the noodles in boiling water according to the instructions on the packet, then drain and rinse under cold water. Drain again and toss with 1 tablespoon of the oil.

2 Slice the meat into thin shreds and top and tail the beans.

3 Heat 3 tablespoons of oil in a preheated wok until hot. Add the noodles and stir-fry for 2–3 minutes with 1 tablespoon soy sauce, then remove to a serving dish. Keep warm.

4 Heat the remaining oil and stir-fry the beans and meat for about 2

minutes. Add the salt, sugar, wine, the remaining soy sauce and about half the spring onions (scallions) to the wok.

5 Blend the meat mixture well and add a little stock if necessary, then pour on top of the noodles, and sprinkle with sesame oil and the remaining spring onions (scallions). Serve hot or cold with or without chilli sauce.

CHOW MEIN

Chow Mein literally means "stir-fried noodles" and is highly popular in the West as well as in China. Almost any ingredient can be added, such as fish, meat, poultry or vegetables. It is very popular for lunch and makes a tasty salad served cold.

STEP 2

STEP 3

STEP 4

STEP 5

NOODLES IN SOUP

Noodles in soup (tang mein) are far more popular than fried noodles (chow mein) in China. You can use different ingredients for the dressing according to taste.

SERVES 4

250 g/8 oz chicken meat, pork fillet (tenderloin), or any other ready-cooked meat
3–4 Chinese dried mushrooms, soaked
125 g/4 oz canned sliced bamboo shoots, rinsed and drained
125 g/4 oz spinach leaves, lettuce hearts or Chinese leaves, shredded
2 spring onions (scallions), finely shredded
250 g/8 oz Chinese egg noodles
about 600 ml/1pint/2¹/₂ cups Chinese Stock (see page 230)
2 tbsp light soy sauce
2 tbsp vegetable oil
1 tsp salt
¹/₂ tsp sugar
2 tsp Chinese rice wine or dry sherry
a few drops sesame oil
1 tsp red chilli oil (optional)

1 Cut the meat into thin shreds. Squeeze dry the soaked mushrooms and discard the hard stalks (stems).

2 Thinly shred the mushrooms, bamboo shoots, spinach leaves and spring onions (scallions).

3 Cook the noodles in boiling water according to the instructions on the packet, then drain and rinse under cold water. Place in a bowl. Bring the stock to the boil, add about 1 tablespoon soy sauce and pour over the noodles. Keep warm.

4 Heat the oil in a pre-heated wok. Add about half of the spring onions (scallions), the meat and the vegetables (mushrooms, bamboo shoots and greens). Stir-fry for 2–3 minutes. Add all the seasonings and blend well.

5 Pour the mixture in the wok over the noodles, garnish with the remaining spring onions (scallions) and serve immediately.

NOODLE SOUP

Noodle soup is wonderfully satisfying and is ideal to serve on cold winter days.

EGG FRIED RICE

The rice used for frying should not be too soft. Ideally, the rice should have been slightly undercooked and left to cool before frying.

STEP 1

SERVES 4

3 eggs
1 tsp salt
2 spring onions (scallions), finely chopped
2–3 tbsp vegetable oil
500 g/1 lb/3 cups cooked rice, well drained and cooled (see note in step 3)
125 g/4 oz cooked peas

1 Lightly beat the eggs with a pinch of salt and 1 tablespoon of the spring onions (scallions).

2 Heat the oil in a preheated wok. Add the eggs and stir until lightly scrambled. (The eggs should only be cooked until they start to set, so they are still moist.)

3 Add the rice and stir to make sure that each grain of rice is separated. Note: the cooked rice should be cool, preferably cold, so that much of the moisture has evaporated. This ensures that the oil will coat the grains of rice and prevent them sticking. Store the cooked rice in the refrigerator until ready to cook. Make sure the oil is really hot before adding the rice, to avoid the rice being saturated with oil otherwise it will be heavy and greasy.

4 Add the remaining salt, spring onions (scallions) and peas. Blend well and serve hot or cold.

STEP 2

PERFECT FRIED RICE

Use rice with a fairly firm texture. Ideally, the raw rice should be soaked in water for a short time before cooking. The two main varieties of rice available are long-grain and short-grain. While it used to be necessary to wash rice, processing now makes this unnecessary. Short-grain Oriental rice can be substituted for long-grain.

Fried rice lends itself to many variations. You may choose to add other vegetables as well as the spring onions (scallions), if desired, as well as prawns (shrimp), ham or chicken.

STEP 3

STEP 4

COMPLETE CHINESE COOKING

The Chinese Diet

THE CHINESE DIET

SPECIAL INGREDIENTS

Here are a few of the
ingredients commonly used in
Chinese cooking. They are
becoming widely available,
particularly in larger supermarkets and health-food stores,
but substitutes can be used for
the more unusual items.

Black beans
Salted fermented soya beans,
available in packets or cans.

Chillies
These can be red or green, and
come in a variety of sizes – the
smaller the chilli, the hotter it
is, and dried chillies are hotter
than fresh. Take care when
handling them, as chilli juice
stings; avoid touching your
eyes and always wash your
hands thoroughly afterwards.
Discard the seeds, as these are
the hottest part.

Chilli oil
A very hot oil flavoured by
chillies and red in colour; use
sparingly. You can make your
own by adding a few dried
chillies to some oil and leaving
them to soak for a few days to
allow the flavour to come out.

China can be divided into four main
regions of cuisine, all of which share a
wealth of foodstuffs and a diversity of
cookery styles. The variety of Chinese
cooking appeals to people in every corner
of the globe, not only because of the
range of unusual and exotic ingredients
but because the daily diet is based largely
on vegetables, rice and fresh noodles.
Fish and meat are normally added for
flavour, and dairy products are not used.
The Chinese diet is considered to be one
of the healthiest in the world.

The art of Chinese cooking is thought
to be particularly ancient. Tea was
known as a drink in China as long as
2,000 years ago. And even today, the
Taoist philosophy of Yin and Yang is still
generally practised, so that balance and
contrast underlies all Chinese cookery
and thus distinguishes it from any other
food culture.

To enjoy the book to the full, take
advantage of these Special Techniques
pages before proceeding with the recipes
and you will soon appreciate the speed
and ease with which Chinese food can be
cooked, whether it is for a complete meal
or simply as an accompaniment to your
normal food.

An overview
China is a vast country situated in a
dominant position in the eastern part of
Asia – in size it is equivalent to Western
Europe. Even though it lies mainly within
the temperate zone both geographically
and climatically, the regions are widely
diverse. From the Tibetan Plateau in the
west (3,600 m/12,000 ft), the country
descends continually eastwards until it
arrives at the Yangtze flood plain. It is the
diversity of the countryside that has
given rise to the wide variety of produce
and the great range of regional cooking
styles. China breaks down into four
distinct regions, each of which has its
own style of cuisine and specialities.

Cantonese (Southern School)
The best-known cuisine in the western
world because of the large numbers of
Chinese that emigrated from Canton to
Europe and America in the nineteenth
century. Also, because Canton was the
first Chinese port opened for trade, it is
the most influenced by foreign contact
and offers the widest variety of food.
Light and subtle flavourings are used and
the food is less fatty than in other
regions. It is famous for its seafood
specialities as well as its sweet and sour
dishes and crispy pork recipes.

Shanghai (Eastern School)
This region is rich in fruit and vegetables,
and is well known for its vegetarian
cuisine as well as its fresh fish. Sugar and
oil are used in large quantities, earning
the area a reputation for rich food.

Szechuan (Western School)
The Szechuan cuisine is characterized by
its dependence on strong flavourings and
hot spices such as red chillies, Szechuan
peppercorns, ginger and garlic.

Peking (Northern School)

The staple food is mainly wheat, corn and maize, rather than rice, with an emphasis on noodles, dumplings and pancakes. Due to the harsh winter, many food products are preserved by drying, smoking or pickling.

The principles of Chinese cooking

What distinguishes Chinese cooking from all other food cultures is the emphasis on the harmonious blending of colour, aroma, flavour and texture, both in a single dish and in a course of dishes for a meal. Balance and contrast are the key words. Chinese cooks from the housewife to the professional chef all work to this yin–yang principle: harmonious balance and contrast by varying the ingredients, cutting shapes, seasonings and cooking methods.

In order to achieve this, two most important factors should be observed, that is, heat and timing – the degree of heat and duration of cooking, which means the right cooking method for the right food. This is why the size and shape of the cut ingredient must, first of all, be suitable for a particular method of cooking. For instance, ingredients for quick stir-frying should be cut into small, thin slices or shreds of uniform size, never into large, thick chunks. This is not just for the sake of appearance, but also because ingredients of the same size and shape require about the same amount of cooking time.

Bear these general points in mind when you cook Chinese food and you will find it surprisingly easy to create delicious dishes that are also a visual delight.

A healthy option

The daily diet of the Chinese is one of the healthiest in the world. Being such a vast country, China encompasses a number of different climates, which gives rise to a wide variety of produce. In addition, the selection of vegetables available in the markets has increased in recent years as China's peasants have been encouraged to grow their own crops.

The vegetarian element

Widespread poverty means that many people are unable to afford meat. Also many follow a vegetarian diet for religious reasons. But even when they have the choice, the Chinese have many reasons for eating more vegetarian food than other kinds. They recognize that a largely vegetarian diet, based on vegetables and carbohydrates (such as rice or noodles) with only a little fish or meat, is the healthiest way to eat, In addition, it is more economical to use the land for growing vegetables and rice than for grazing livestock, as the crops will feed far more people than the livestock will.

EATING THE CHINESE WAY

Chinese cooking is one of the oldest known cuisines, and its influence has spread throughout the world. Its essence is harmony of flavour, colour and texture. The recipes in this book have been designed to achieve exactly this. They are quick and simple to prepare and they mostly use ingredients obtainable from supermarkets. Occasionally, you may need to visit a Chinese food store to find one or two ingredients. Some of the

Lemon grass

An aromatic herb, available as fresh stems or dried as powder. Chop or slice the lower part of the stem to use.

Lily flowers

Also known as golden needles, these are dried lily-flower buds. Soak in water before use.

Lotus leaves

Leaves of the lotus plant. They are very large and sold dried. Soak in hot water before use. These are often used as a shell in which other ingredients are cooked, such as steamed rice.

Noodles

Made from rice, pulses or wheat. There is a large variety available, all of which can be interchanged in recipes. Cook according to packet instructions as times vary from one type to another.

Sesame seeds

Add texture and a nutty flavour. Dry-fry to add colour and accentuate the flavour.

CHINESE STOCK

This basic stock is used not only as the basis for soup-making, but also for general use in Chinese cooking.

MAKES 2.5 LITRES/4 PINTS/ 10 CUPS

750 g/1¹/₂ lb chicken pieces
750 g/1¹/₂ lb pork spare ribs
3.75 litres/6 pints/15 cups cold water
3-4 pieces ginger root, crushed
3-4 spring onions (scallions), each tied into a knot
3-4 tbsp Chinese rice wine or dry sherry

1. Trim off excess fat from the chicken and spare ribs; chop them into large pieces.

2. Place the chicken and pork in a large pan with water; add the ginger and spring onion (scallion) knots.

3. Bring to the boil, and skim off the scum. Reduce heat and simmer uncovered for at least 2-3 hours.

4. Strain the stock, discarding the chicken, pork, ginger and spring onions (scallions); add the wine and return to the boil, simmer for 2-3 minutes.

Refrigerate the stock. When cool, it will keep for up to 4-5 days. Alternatively, it can be frozen in small containers and be defrosted as required.

recipes have been adapted for the vegetarian from traditional Chinese recipes, and others are vegetarian dishes that have been developed to suit the Western kitchen.

Meal times in China are often family gatherings, at which many different dishes are served. A wide range of ingredients is used, but the different flavours of the many dishes are always made to work together. The meal is served all at once, including the soup. Unlike the Western convention, the Chinese never serve an individual dish to each person; all the dishes on the table are shared.

Preparing a Chinese meal

When planning a menu for this kind of shared meal, allow one dish per person. For example, if you are cooking for only two or three people, serve one main dish with one vegetable side dish and one rice or noodle dish, plus a soup if desired. For an informal meal for four to six people, serve four dishes plus soup and rice; for a formal dinner for approximately the same number of people, allow a range of six to eight dishes. Always increase the number of dishes rather than the quantity of ingredients when cooking for many people, as this will give more variety and contrast of taste, colour and flavour on the table.

Do not choose too many dishes that need a lot of last-minute preparation or have to be served immediately, such as stir-fries. Vary the dishes so that some may be prepared in advance, and then you too can enjoy the meal and not spend all evening in the kitchen.

GLOSSARY OF INGREDIENTS

The list covers the most commonly used ingredients in Chinese cooking. These ingredients are becoming much more widely available, particularly in the supermarkets, health food shops and Chinese stores. Substitutes can often be used for the more unusual ingredients.

Baby sweetcorn (corn) Baby corn cobs have a wonderfully sweet fragrance and flavour, and irresistible texture. They are available both fresh and canned.

Bamboo shoots Available in cans only. Once opened, the contents may be kept in fresh water in a covered jar in the refrigerator for up to a week.

Bean-sprouts Fresh bean-sprouts, from mung or soya beans, are widely available from Oriental stores and supermarkets. They can be kept in the refrigerator for two to three days.

Bean sauce Available in black or yellow, bean sauce is made from crushed salted soya beans mixed with flour and spices (such as ginger or chilli) to make a thickish paste. It is used for flavouring dishes or as a condiment. The sauce is sold in cans or jars and once opened should be stored in the refrigerator.

Chilli bean sauce Fermented bean paste mixed with hot chillies and other seasonings. Sold in jars, some sauces are quite mild, but others are very hot. You will have to try out the various brands to see which one is to your taste.

Chinese leaves Also known as Chinese cabbage, there are two widely available varieties to be found in supermarkets and greengrocers. The most commonly seen one is a pale green colour and has a tightly wrapped, elongated head – about two-thirds of the cabbage is stem, which has a crunchy texture. The other variety has a shorter, fatter head with curlier, pale yellow or green leaves, also with white stems.

Dried Chinese mushrooms (shiitake) Highly fragrant dried mushrooms which add a special flavour to Chinese dishes. There are many different varieties, but shiitake are the best. They are not cheap, but a small amount will go a long way, and they will keep indefinitely in an air-tight jar. Soak them in warm water for 20–30 minutes (or in cold water for several hours), squeeze dry and discard the hard stalks (stems) before use.

Coriander Fresh coriander leaves, also known as Chinese parsley or cilantro, have a distinctive flavour. Coriander is widely used in Chinese cooking. It can be chopped and added to sauces and stuffing. The feathery leaves make an attractive garnish. Parsley can be used as a substitute.

Egg noodles There are many varieties of noodles in China, ranging from flat, broad ribbons to long, narrow strands. Both dried and fresh noodles are readily available.

Five-spice powder A mixture of star anise, fennel seeds, cloves, cinnamon bark and Szechuan pepper. It is very pungent so should be used sparingly. It will keep in an airtight container indefinitely.

Garlic A primary seasoning in Chinese food that not only adds flavour but has health-giving properties. Garlic may be chopped, crushed or pickled and is very often used in sauces and stuffings. Store garlic in a cool, dry area, not in the fridge where it will go mouldy.

Ginger root Fresh ginger root, sold by the weight, should be peeled and then sliced, finely chopped or shredded before use. It will keep for several weeks in a dry, cool place. Dried ginger powder is no substitute.

Oils The most commonly used oil in Chinese cooking is peanut oil, which, because of its light flavour, is especially good in stir-frying and deep frying. Rape or sunflower oils are also popular, while butter is never used, and lard and chicken fat only occasionally.

Oyster sauce A thickish soy-based sauce used as a flavouring in Cantonese cooking. Sold in bottles, it will keep in the refrigerator for months.

Plum sauce Plum sauce has a unique, fruity flavour – a sweet and sour sauce with a difference.

Rice vinegar There are two basic types of rice vinegar. Red vinegar is made from fermented rice and has a distinctive dark colour and depth of flavour. White

CORNFLOUR (CORNSTARCH) PASTE

Cornflour (cornstarch) paste is made by mixing 1 part cornflour (cornstarch) with about 1.5 parts of cold water. Stir until smooth. Use to thicken sauces.

PRAWNS (SHRIMP) WITH DIP SAUCE

300 g/10 oz raw prawns (shrimp), defrosted if frozen
1 tsp salt
1 litre/1 3/4 pints/4 cups water
2 spring onions (scallions), shredded
2–3 slices ginger root, shredded
2 green or red chillies, deseeded and finely shredded
1 tbsp light soy sauce
1 tbsp red rice vinegar
1 tsp sesame seed oil

1. Poach the prawns (shrimp) in boiling, salted water for 1 minute, then turn off the heat. Leave to stand for 1 minute, remove with a slotted spoon and drain on paper towels.

2. Place the spring onions (scallions), ginger and chillies in a small heatproof bowl. Heat the oil and pour into the bowl. Add the soy sauce, vinegar and sesame oil and stir well.

3. Shell the prawns (shrimp), leaving the tails, and arrange on a serving dish. Serve with the dip sauce.

PLAIN RICE

Use long-grain or patna rice, or better still, try fragrant Thai rice.

SERVES 4

250 g/8 oz/1¹/₄ cups long-grain rice
about 200 ml/7 fl oz/1 cup cold water
pinch of salt
¹/₂ tsp oil (optional)

1. Wash and rinse the rice just once. Place the rice in a saucepan and add enough water so that there is no more than 2 cm/½ in of water above the surface of the rice.

2. Bring to the boil, add salt and oil (if using), and stir to prevent the rice sticking to the bottom of the pan.

3. Reduce the heat to very, very low. Cover and cook for 15–20 minutes.

4. Remove from the heat and let stand, covered, for 10 minutes or so. Fluff up the rice with a fork or spoon before serving.

vinegar is stronger in flavour as it is distilled from rice wine.

Rice wine Chinese rice wine, made from glutinous rice, is also known as 'Yellow wine' (*Huang jiu* or *chiew* in Chinese), because of its golden colour. The best variety, from south-east China, is called Shao Hsing or Shaoxing. A good dry or medium sherry can be an acceptable substitute.

Sesame oil Aromatic oil sold in bottles and widely used as a finishing touch, added to dishes just before serving. The refined yellow sesame oil sold in Middle Eastern stores is not so aromatic, has less flavour and therefore is not a very satisfactory substitute.

Sherry If rice wine is difficult to obtain, a good quality, dry pale sherry can be used instead. Cream or sweet sherry should not be substituted.

Soy sauce Sold in bottles or cans, this popular Chinese sauce is used both for cooking and at the table. Light soy sauce has more flavour than the sweeter, dark soy sauce, which gives the food a rich, reddish colour.

Straw mushrooms Grown on beds of rice straw, hence the name, straw mushrooms have a pleasant slippery texture, and a subtle taste. Canned straw mushrooms should be rinsed and drained after opening.

Szechuan peppercorns Also known as *farchiew*, these are wild reddish-brown peppercorns from Szechuan. More aromatic but less hot than either white or black peppercorns, they do give a unique and delicious flavour to a variety of dishes.

Szechuan preserved vegetable This is a speciality of Szechuan province. It is the root of a special variety of the mustard, green pickled in salt and hot chilli. Sold in cans, once opened it can be stored in a sealed jar in the refrigerator for months.

Tofu (bean curd) This custard-like preparation of puréed and pressed yellow soya beans is exceptionally high in protein. Tofu has a distinctive texture but a bland flavour. It is usually sold in two forms: in cakes about 7.5 cm/ 3 inches square and 2.5 cm/1 inch thick or as a semi-thick jelly. There is also a dried form, which is sold in Oriental and health food stores. For solid tofu, use a sharp knife to cut the required amount into cubes or shreds. Cook carefully as it will break up if stirred too much. Tofu will keep for a few days if put in a container, submerged in water and placed in a refrigerator.

Water chestnuts The roots of the plant *Heleocharis tuberosa*. Also known as horse's hooves in China on account of their appearance before the skin is peeled off. They are available fresh or in cans. Canned water chestnuts retain only part of the texture, and even less of the flavour, of fresh ones. Will keep for about a month in the refrigerator in a covered jar, changing the water every two or three days.

Wood ears Also known as cloud ears, this is a dried black fungus. Sold in plastic bags in Oriental stores, it should be soaked in cold or warm water for 20 minutes, then rinsed in fresh water before use. It has a crunchy texture and mild but subtle flavour. Fresh 'Jews ears' are a good substitute.

Wonton skins or wrappers These are made from flour, egg and water. They can be deep fried and served with a dipping sauce, or filled prior to deep frying, steaming or boiling. Buy them ready-made or make your own. Layers of filo pastry make a reasonable substitute. They can be kept frozen for up to six months.

ADDED EXTRAS

In addition to the staple ingredients shown in this section, there are delicious Chinese sauces you can add while cooking your dish, or just before serving it, which will enhance its authentic flavour. Here are some suggestions:

Hoisin sauce Also known as barbecue sauce, this is made from soy beans, sugar, flour, vinegar, salt, garlic, chilli and sesame seed oil. Sold in cans or jars, it will keep in the refrigerator for several months.

Chilli sauce Very hot sauce made from chillis, vinegar, sugar and salt. Usually sold in bottles and should be used sparingly in cooking or as a dip. Tabasco sauce can be a substitute if you do not happen to have the real thing.

GARNISHES

Chinese food should always be pleasing to the eye as well as the palate. The dishes can be intricately decorated with delicately cut vegetables, adding colour as well as a finishing touch. The garnishes can be as simple or elaborate as you wish, depending on time and patience. The more simple garnishes could be sprigs of fresh or chopped herbs such as coriander (cilantro), chervil or chives, shreds of spring onion (scallion), chilli, lemon zest or radish, or twists of lime or lemon. Some more elaborate garnishes are described below. Experiment with both for the best results.

Cucumber fans Cut a piece of cucumber about 7.5 cm/3 inches long and divide this in half lengthways. Lay a piece of cucumber cut side down and, using a small, sharp knife, cut thin slices along the length to within 1 cm/½ inch of the end. Carefully turn alternate slices over in half and tuck in. Place in iced water until required.

Carrot flowers Peel the carrot. Using a sharp knife, make about five or six tiny V-shaped cuts along the length. Then cut into slices: the V-shapes will ensure each slice looks like a flower petal.

Fresh chilli flowers Trim the tip of the chilli but do not remove the skin. Make four cuts lengthways from the stem of the chilli to the tip to make four sections. Remove and discard any seeds. Soak the chillis in cold water – they will flower in the water.

CHINESE FRUIT SALAD

The Chinese do not usually have desserts to finish off a meal, except at banquets and special occasions. Sweet dishes are usually served in between main meals as snacks, but fruit is refreshing at the end of a big meal.

250 g/8 oz/1 cup rock candy or crystal sugar
600 ml/1 pint/2½ cups boiling water
1 large honeydew melon
4–5 different fruits, such as pineapple, grapes, banana, mango, lychees or kiwi fruit

1. Dissolve the rock candy in the boiling water, then leave to cool.

2. Slice 2.5 cm/1 in off the top of the melon and scoop out the flesh, discarding the seeds. Cut the flesh into small chunks. Prepare the other fruits and cut into small chunks.

3. Fill the melon shell with the fruits and the syrup. Cover with clingfilm (plastic wrap) and chill for at least 2 hours. Serve on a bed of crushed ice.

EXTRA GARNISHES

Prawn (shrimp) crackers These consist of compressed slivers of prawn (shrimp) and flour paste. They expand into large, translucent crisps when deep fried.

Radish flowers Trim each end of the radish. Using a sharp knife, make 'V' cuts around the top and remove the cut parts to expose the whites of the radish.

Radish roses For radish roses, trim the ends, then hold the knife flat to the radish skin and make short vertical cuts around the sides, as if you were shaving off the outer skin, but without detaching each 'petal'. Plunge straight into iced water.

Tomato roses For tomato roses, peel off the skin of a tomato using a sharp knife in one long strip. Curl the skin into a circle.

EQUIPMENT

There are only a few basic implements in the Chinese *batterie de cuisine* that are considered essential in order to achieve the best results. Equivalent equipment is available in a Western kitchen, but Chinese utensils are of an ancient design, usually made of inexpensive materials, have been in continuous use for thousands of years and do serve a special function. Their more sophisticated and expensive Western counterparts prove rather inadequate in contrast.

Chinese cleaver Good, strong, sharp kitchen knives are more than adequate but it is worth trying to work with a Chinese cleaver. The wide blade looks clumsy, but the corner of the blade can do anything the point of a knife can do. A cleaver is the best thing for slicing, shredding, chopping and dicing. In addition, the wide blade can carry the chopped ingredients from the board to the cooking pot.

Cleavers vary in weight and thickness of blade; the heavier type, for chopping through bones, is used a lot in Chinese cooking, while the lighter, sharper type is ideal for delicate, precision work. It is best to work with the cleaver on a wooden board as the surface is not slippery and is therefore safer to use.

Chopping block Traditionally, the Chinese always worked on a chopping block. This is a cross-section of a tree-trunk about 40 cm/16 inches across and 15 cm/6 inches thick, and is sturdy and porous. It is, however, difficult to obtain.

Wok The round-bottomed iron wok conducts and retains heat evenly, and because of its shape, the ingredients always return to the centre, where the heat is most intense, however vigorously you stir. The wok is also ideal for deep frying – its conical shape requires far less oil than the flat-bottomed deep fryer, and has more depth (which means more heat) and more cooking surface (which means more food can be cooked at one go). Besides being a frying-pan (skillet), a wok is also used for braising, steaming, boiling and poaching etc. – in other words, the whole spectrum of Chinese cooking methods can be executed in one single utensil.

It is essential that a new iron wok is seasoned properly before use. Prepare it by washing thoroughly in hot water and detergent then drying it well. To season, put it over a gentle heat and, when the metal heats up, wipe over the entire inner surface with a pad of paper towels (kitchen paper) that you have first dipped in oil. Repeat with fresh oiled paper until the paper stays clean.

Steamers Steaming can be done in any covered pot large enough to take a plate which is placed on a rack to hold it above the boiling water. There has to be space for the steam to circulate. The food is put on the plate and a well-fitting lid put on top. A wok with its own lid will serve very well. The traditional Chinese steamer is made of bamboo and is particularly well-adapted to steaming as the gaps in the bamboo allow excess steam to escape; the modern version is made of aluminium.

Frying spoons These spoons of fine wire mesh are useful for lifting small pieces of food out of the oil, as is a large wire spoon that can lift an entire fish out.

Ladle and spatula Wok sets usually consist of a pair of stirrers in the form of a ladle and spatula. Of the two, the flat ladle or scooper (as it is sometimes called) is more versatile. It is used by the Chinese cook for adding ingredients and seasonings to the wok, besides being a stirring implement.

Strainers There are two basic types of strainers – one is made of copper or steel wire with long bamboo handles, the other of perforated metal (iron or stainless steel). Several different sizes are available.

Chopsticks Does Chinese food taste any better when eaten with chopsticks? This is not merely an aesthetic question, but also a practical point, partly because all Chinese food is prepared in such a way that it is easily picked up by chopsticks.

Learning to use chopsticks is quite easy – simply place one chopstick in the hollow between thumb and index finger and rest its lower end below the first joint of the third finger. This chopstick remains stationary. Hold the other chopstick between the tips of the the index and middle finger, steady its upper half against the base of the index finger, and use the tip of the thumb to keep it in place. To pick up food, move the upper chopstick with index and middle fingers. When eating rice and other difficult-to-hold foods, it is better to lift the bowl to the chin and then push the food into the mouth using the chopsticks as a type of shovel, as the Chinese do.

THE ART OF TEA DRINKING

Tea has been known as a drink in China certainly for more than 2,000 years and probably much earlier. However, it was not until the eighth century AD that tea became a common drink, popular with all classes of people. Today, tea drinking is a part of everyday life in China and a pot of strong tea is kept warm all day to provide a regular supply.

When to serve tea
Tea is unlikely to be drunk during the actual meal, as it is generally the custom to place a bowl of clear soup on the table instead for the duration of the meal. Tea is then served at the end of the meal as it is considered to be both refreshing and invigorating.

A Chinese ritual
To the tea connoisseur, tea drinking is almost a mystical ritual. Ideally, preparing tea should be carried out under immaculate and tranquil conditions. The setting is especially important and should be as peaceful as possible; in fact, the ideal spot is considered to be on a mountain so that, as an additional benefit, mountain water is used for the tea. For the connoisseur, the tradition of tea drinking is, as it has always been through the ages, akin to a religious ritual and a return to nature and purity.

DIPPING SAUCES
Traditional sauces for Chinese food include the following:

SWEET & SOUR SAUCE

A tasty sweet and sour sauce which goes well with many deep fried foods. Store in a well-sealed jar in the refrigerator. It will keep well.

2 tbsp ginger marmalade
2 tbsp orange marmalade
1/4 tsp salt
1 tbsp white rice vinegar (or cider vinegar)
1 tbsp hot water

Combine all the ingredients in a small bowl, mixing well. Serve in a small bowl.

SALT & PEPPER SAUCE

A roasted salt and pepper mixture made with Szechuan peppercorns is found throughout China as a dip for deep-fried foods. The dry-roasting method brings out all the flavours of the peppercorns.

2 oz/ 50 g Szechuan peppercorns
3 oz/ 75 g coarse sea salt

Put a heavy frying-pan (skillet) over medium heat. Add the peppercorns and the salt and stir-fry until the mixture begins to brown. Remove the pan (skillet) from the heat and let the mixture cool. Grind the mixture in a grinder or with a pestle and mortar.

SPRING ONION (SCALLION) SAUCE

Heated oil poured over the seasonings brings out their full flavour. The sauce goes well with meat and poultry dishes.

*3 tbsp spring onions (scallions),
   chopped finely*
*3 tbsp fresh ginger root, grated
   finely*
2 tsp salt
1 tsp light soy sauce
3 tbsp oil (peanut or sunflower)

1. Place the spring onions (scallions), ginger root, salt and soy sauce in a small heatproof bowl.

2. Put the oil into a small saucepan and heat over a moderate heat until it begins to smoke.

3. Remove the oil from the heat and pour over the seasonings. Leave the sauce to stand for at least 2–3 hours before using, to allow the flavours to blend.

COOKING METHODS

Chinese food generally takes much longer to prepare than it does to cook, so it is very important to prepare each dish as much in advance as possible. Have all the vegetables chopped and sauces blended before you start cooking.

The ingredients should be cut into small, uniformly sized pieces. This ensures that the food will cook evenly. The prepared food is often cooked very briefly over a high heat, which seals in the natural juices and helps to preserve the nutrients. This short cooking time leaves the end product more succulent and preserves its texture as well as its natural flavours and colours. Shredding vegetables thinly and slicing them diagonally ensures fast cooking, as it increases the area that comes into contact with the hot oil.

Stir-frying

This is the method of cooking most commonly associated with Chinese cuisine. The correct piece of equipment for this is a wok, although any large frying-pan (skillet) or heavy saucepan will do. It is best to use a wok (described on page 234) as it gives the best results.

Stir-frying with a wok is a very healthy way to cook, as it uses very little oil and preserves the nutrients in the food as they cook for such a short time. It is very important that the wok is very hot before you begin to cook. This can be tested by holding your hand flat about 7.5 cm/ 3 inches over the base of the interior, when you will feel the heat radiating

from it. The success of stir-frying lies in having the wok at just the right temperature, and in ensuring correct timing when cooking the food.

Before cooking commences, ensure that all the required ingredients are prepared – chopped, diced and sliced – and so ready to be added to the wok the instant the oil is the right heat. Cooking at too low a temperature or for too long will cause loss of quality.

Add a small amount of oil to the wok and heat it, then add, in stages, the various ingredients to be cooked – those requiring longer cooking go in first, while those that require only very little cooking go in last.

The ingredients should be stirred constantly for a very short time using a long-handled metal or wooden spoon or flat scoop. Constantly stirring ensures that all the ingredients come into contact with the hot oil so the natural juices of the food are sealed in, leaving it crisp and colourful. It also ensures that all the ingredients are evenly cooked. Stir-fried dishes look and taste best when served immediately.

Cleaning a wok

Clean the wok after each use by washing it with water, using a mild detergent if necessary, and a soft cloth or brush. Do not scrub or use any abrasive cleaner as this will scratch the surface. Dry thoroughly with paper towels or over a low heat, then wipe the surface all over with a little oil. This forms a sealing layer to protect the surface of the wok from moisture and thus helps to prevent it from rusting.

Steaming

This is another very popular Chinese method of cooking. The piece of equipment the Chinese use is a bamboo steamer. As these are not airtight, they allow a certain amount of steam to escape, preventing any condensation from forming on the lid. They are designed to stand one on top of another, enabling you to cook several dishes at the same time. Bamboo steamers can be bought at Chinese speciality shops or good cookware shops in a range of sizes.

There are two methods of steaming; in the first the food is arranged on a plate or bowl which is then put inside a steamer on the perforated rack and placed over a large pot of boiling water or put inside a wok. The steam passes through the steamer and cooks the food. Larger items of food such as dumplings can be placed straight on to the rack or laid on cabbage or soaked lotus leaves, which prevents the food from falling through and adds extra flavour. Alternatively, the bowl of ingredients can be immersed partway into the boiling water and the food is cooked partly by the boiling water and partly by the steam it produces.

Deep-frying

Use a wok, a deep-fryer or a heavy-based saucepan. When deep-frying in a wok, use enough oil to give a depth of about 5 cm/2 inches and heat it over a moderate heat until you can see a faint haze of smoke rising before gently lowering in the food to be fried. Make sure the oil is up to temperature before adding the food: the hot oil should cook the food quickly on the outside, sealing it and forming a barrier around it, which prevents the food from acting like a sponge and becoming soggy and greasy, which is what will happen if the oil is not hot enough.

Before frying the food, ensure that it is dry to prevent the oil from splattering. If the food is in a marinade, let it drain well and, if it is in batter, wait for it to stop dripping. Oil, once it has been strained, can be reused up to three times, but only for the same type of food.

Cook the food in small batches so as not to overcrowd the wok or pan, as this can reduce the temperature of the oil, and lead to unevenly cooked food. Always remove the food from the oil with a perforated spoon and drain on paper towels to absorb any excess oil.

Braising and red braising

This method is similar to Western braising and is generally used with the tougher cuts of meat and the firmer vegetables. The ingredients are stir-fried until lightly brown, stock is added and brought to the boil and then the heat is reduced to simmering until cooking is complete. Red braising uses the same method of cooking but the food is braised in a reddish-brown liquid, such as soy sauce. This sauce can be reused.

Cooking with chopsticks

These long wooden or plastic sticks are not only used for eating but also for cooking, as they are an excellent tool to stir, whip and beat the ingredients during preparation. They can be bought in most cookshops and from many Chinese restaurants.

CHINESE WINE

Chinese wine is mostly made with fermented rice, which gives the wine a very different flavour from wine made with grapes. It is an acquired taste. The best-known Chinese wine is called Shaoxing, which is also used in cooking.

OTHER SUITABLE WINES

Many European and New World wines blend well with Chinese food, particularly the light, dry whites and lighter Burgundy-style reds.

INDEX